EXPLORE YOUR PSYCHIC WORLD

EXPLORE YOUR PSYCHIC WORLD

*Ambrose A. Worrall and Olga N. Worrall
with Will Oursler*

HARPER & ROW, PUBLISHERS
New York, Evanston, and London

LIBRARY OF CONGRESS CATALOG CARD NUMBER: 79-85062

Contents

	Preface	vii
	Introduction	ix
1	You and Your Universe	1
2	You the Clairvoyant	13
3	An Aura of Gold	29
4	Laws and Superlaws	44
5	Body and Soul	60
6	A Time for Silence	76
7	Force Fields of Healing	85
8	Possessed by What?	103
9	Shadows and Ghosts	113
10	Search and Research	125
11	Road Signs	136
12	Meanings	142

Preface

Wainwright House in Rye, New York, since becoming the Laymen's Movement headquarters in 1951, has brought together more than ten thousand men and women in quest of a greater understanding of God.

The Laymen's Movement, an international nonsectarian association, was founded in 1941 by a small group of businessmen. Its purpose is to help each member develop his inner resources and thereby contribute meaningfully to the lives of others.

Explore Your Psychic World is a product of the deeper search as carried on by the Commission for the Study of Healing, one of the many active Wainwright House groups. It is based on a series of six seminars on spiritual healing conducted by Olga and Ambrose Worrall in the fall and winter of 1967-68.

The Commission for the Study of Healing, under the leadership of its chairman, Dr. Robert W. Laidlaw, is continuing its investigations and is currently carrying out an even deeper inquiry into the subject of spiritual healing.

WEYMAN C. HUCKABEE
Secretary of The Laymen's Movement
and Director of Wainwright House

Introduction

> Miracles do not happen in contradiction to nature, but only in contradiction to that which is known to us of nature.
>
> St. Augustine

In its statement of policy and purpose the Commission for the Study of Healing of the Laymen's Movement has declared the following:

> The Commission for the Study of Healing of the Laymen's Movement believes that the phenomena encompassed in the term "spiritual healing" are a manifestation of the working of law. This is a higher echelon of law which at times seemingly transcends the biological laws in regard to healing such as are known to medicine today. It is the purpose of the Commission to carry out investigations which will add to our knowledge of how this higher echelon of law operates. We already are aware of the fact that a complexity of factors contributes to the successful operation of these laws, factors which involve both the "healer" and the "healed." We are currently involved in studying and analyzing such factors.
>
> Our work has included the study of selected patients while under active treatment, as well as seminars in which discussions between doctors and healers focus on both subjective and objective factors which make for success in the healer's work.

It will be noted in the following report of the seminars held with Olga and Ambrose Worrall that the discussions emphasized this point of view.

The doctors who participated in these deliberations are to be congratulated for their openness of mind in examining concepts so at variance with their basic medical training. This is in marked contrast to the attitude of the medical profession as a whole as described by Dr. Newton J. Bigelow, former Commissioner of the New York State Department of Mental Hygiene and currently editor of *The Psychiatric Quarterly* and *Psychiatric Quarterly Supplement*. In an editorial by him, which appeared in the *Psychiatric Quarterly* in April, 1949, he stated:

> Parapsychological phenomena (psychic phenomena) although commanding increased psychiatric attention of late, appear to have met more scorn than indignation. . . . [Yet] they contain implications of vast importance for both theory and treatment. . . . We suggest . . . that psychiatrists and others in a position to make observations may now well endeavor to observe more carefully and report more systematically than they have been used to doing. We suggest that, as a preliminary, they endeavor to familiarize themselves with what has been done and what is being done inside and outside our own specialty in the way of sober, scientific study of parapsychological phenomena.
>
> . . . We think, in these days of accelerated progress and heightened controversy, of bold advance and bitter recrimination . . . that we could bear with a few heroic qualities. . . . another time has come when we need to take particular care not to "allow authority, conceit, habit, or the fear of ridicule to make us hostile to truth."

Explore Your Psychic World gives the highlights of the Worrall seminars. Every word at these seminars was recorded on tape and transcribed into typewritten form. From this typewritten material

Will Oursler has selected the direct quotations that, with minor editing, constitute the body of this book. His skillfully interspersed comments and explanatory material add pace and clarity.

The full verbatim transcript of these seminars is on file with other parapsychological material in Wainwright House. Serious students wishing to examine this transcript on the premises will be granted permission to do so.

The Commission for the Study of Healing is grateful to Mr. John Hewitt of the Wainwright House staff for the many hours which he spent in supervising the tape recordings, and especially wishes to thank Miss Olive Freeman, its research assistant, for her invaluable help in preparing all of this material for publication.

ROBERT W. LAIDLAW, M.D.

Chairman

Commission for the Study of Healing

EXPLORE YOUR PSYCHIC WORLD

1

You and Your Universe

Before the beginning, God brought his perfect law into being.

This was Causation, the act of causing, the introduction of an agency by which an effect is produced. The perfect law makes possible all creation. The perfect law is immutable law; it cannot change, nor can it be changed; it works without fail, always; it cannot be circumvented or ignored; without it there could be nothing, for there would be neither observer nor anything to observe. . . . God has no magnitude, he exists in the realm of no dimensions. He is . . . in perfect balance.

God is Universal Mind. Universal Mind has no dimensions, yet it contains every possible idea, every conceivable form or pattern . . . all that is knowable.

God is Universal Will. Universal Will is the power responsible for creation. . . .

Causation is in the realm of no dimensions; creation is in the realm of dimensions. Causation cannot be perceived; creation is perceptible. Creation is impossible without motion; motion requires space. Motion operating in space requires time. Space and time are the byproducts of motion. Motion, space, and time are the essentials of creation.

Creative motion is in wave form. The type of wave form is dependent upon the selected pure idea. The intensity of the wave form is dependent upon the universal will. . . . Life is God expressing himself through creation.

The individual is nondimensional. He is the image of God. . . .

The speaker was Ambrose Worrall, scientist and engineer, for many years an executive in one of America's great aircraft manufacturing companies and later consultant for one of the largest industrial-electrical manufacturers in the nation. Both Ambrose and his wife Olga have gifts of healing seership. Neither, however, has ever used these gifts for commercial reasons. Olga and her husband have used their forces almost entirely in association with organized religious-psychological-healing clinics in churches in Baltimore, Maryland.

Each of these individuals has known clairvoyant experiences since their earliest childhood—Ambrose in his native England and Olga in her native city of Cleveland, Ohio. It was in Cleveland that Olga and Ambrose met and were married. Shortly thereafter the couple moved to Baltimore.

One example of the problems of the psychically gifted occurred during their courtship. They were young people in love. Somehow this young love set up a roadblock; neither had the least idea of the other's paranormal gifts. And for many months before their marriage they dared not tell each other of their psychic interests nor of the episodes they had experienced since early childhood.

Ultimately, before the marriage, they did reveal and discuss these extranormal episodes and were startled to discover that their experiences were closely parallel, even to the fact that in both cases their parents ordered them—as children—to stop talking about the so-called "people" they saw or heard in their rooms and homes. These "people" and "voices," the parents insisted, were entirely out of their children's imaginations.

Neither the parents nor the children in either instance had heard of the other at that time. Further, they were separated by thousands of miles of land mass and ocean.

But it was because of the extraordinary experiences of the Worralls over many years, particularly their unequaled record in spiritual healing, much of which is told in their book, *The Gift of Healing*, that Wainwright House and the Laymen's Movement invited them to hold the seminars at this important center of religious and para-normal research.

Those in attendence were no mere curiosity seekers nor sensa-tion hunters. They were psychiatrists, internists, surgeons, students of psychology and parapsychology, scientists, engineers, electrical authorities, medical school professors.

The gathering at the sessions in the quiet charm of Wainwright House was a cross section of professional, gifted individuals inter-ested in objectively exploring in depth the evidence for and against the varieties of paranormal experience.

It was Ambrose, in a gentle, calm voice, tinged with a middle English accent, who began the discussion. In his opening state-ment, he sought to bring into perspective the philosophical-scientific-religious elements involved in this quest for spiritual discovery. He outlined what these elements mean—and can mean—for our lives.

The range of topics that were open for discussion are of increasing significance to all humanity. In today's expanding awareness all mankind is becoming involved with these questions. Even the Rus-sians have been conducting wide-roving experiments into psychic questions—investigations carried out with their usual secrecy. Should the Communist investigators discover God empirically, they might find themselves in a grave situation with government au-thorities.

Ambrose, at the outset of the opening discussion, reminded the gathering that man has not only a natural but also a spiritual body:

We have to keep that in mind. Man being created in the image of God, possesses mind, will, and creative power. This does not make man equal to God but makes him like unto God. The essence of God is in man, but man's power is limited by his sense of separateness from God and from his fellow men. Man is not capable of causation; he is capable of creation by using the universal law of creation, which is the perfect law. Man's mind is a part of the Universal Mind in which all knowledge is stored. All knowledge is available to the man who over-comes the barriers that separate him from God, the barriers erected by himself. These same barriers separate man from man and prevent him from obeying the important commandment, "Love one another." Or again, "Love thy neighbor as thyself. . . ."

There are stimuli that man is conscious of and which are com-monly known. These enter his consciousness through the five physical senses: seeing, hearing, touching, smelling, and tasting. But there are other excitants which are not so widely known or understood by the masses. These are active in the unseen realm of forces. . . .

The part of man that does not think is a part of the Universal Mind which has no need to think. It already knows the answers to all questions; the solution to all problems; how the creative law will work under any set of conditions; and it is never confused. . . .

Man must realize that stimuli come from sources external to him-self. Therefore, he must not expect to receive unadulterated ideas from an outward search. Introspection, looking within, true self-examination, this should be the direction. And during this search he must not be conscious of the outer turmoil but, by seeking silence within, gradually but surely must withdraw from the outer world of sensation and enter this realm of intuition which precedes that deep silence out of which come the ideas he needs in a pure state. This is the silence in which God dwells. . . .

Ambrose the engineer, the healer, the mystic, ranged wide in his presentation of the fields of inquiry, the meanings into which he and Olga and the group later delved; the questions of psychic forces, possession, auras, the role of silence, the whole area of reli-gious or spiritual healing. Ambrose spoke of the roads by which one can approach these varied and often elusive points—the diverse approaches of religion, psychology, philosophy, pure science. And of the individual, the average citizen of our time, searching amid new and often bewildering theorems and theories for answers in our own individual lives.

At times this somewhat stocky spokesman of the psyche spoke with extraordinary earthy symbolism:

By his desires man can create conditions beneficial to mankind—or detrimental. Being part of the whole, he should be wise enough to know that he must be concerned with his feet as much as his head. If a man's feet hurt, he hurts all over. And so it is with humanity. The downtrodden ones are the feet. . . .

And a moment later in this presentation he moved to a wholly different realm:

Man cannot change the perfect law, which is the creative law. Man can be influenced by external stimuli received through the five senses, and from those received in other ways than through the organs of sense. Man is to a large extent the author of his own environment. That which is imperceptible is the source of all that can be perceived.

In the group dialogue that followed, the gathering began to probe specific meanings and implications, salient points of these facets of the paranormal:

Dr. Robert W. Laidlaw: When you speak about a man having two bodies, a physical body and a spiritual, where do you feel that man's aura comes into this concept?

AW: It is with the spiritual body. When the spiritual body occupies the physical body, the aura is seen around the physical body because the spiritual body is a tenant at that particular time.

Dr. Thelma Arthur:[1] Does the aura change if the physical body is injured or ill?

AW: Yes! The color of the aura changes—it becomes less bright. The lines of the etheric field radiate outward from the body in health, but droop in sickness or injury at the location of the trouble. Dr. Michael Ash[2] said that he could see leaks in the aura at the seat of trouble. The drooping lines do give the appearance of something leaking out of the body.

Dr. Laidlaw: As an engineer, Ambrose, you'd be interested in

1. Doctor of medicine; clinician and researcher in cytomorphology.

2. An English healer, who has participated in Wainwright House healing sessions.

knowing that one of the trustees of the American Society for Psychical Research and myself talked with the top electronics engineer of RCA in regard to a research study of the aura and he feels that instrumentation, electronic instrumentation, has proceeded to the point where it can be so set up as to make the human aura visible in color on a modified TV screen. Dr. Gardner and I were talking about this on the way up.

AW: We ought to found a society and call it the parascientific society for all those things alongside of science which science doesn't embrace in its present scope of interest.

Question (from unidentified voice): I want to ask you a question, Ambrose. Is the eye the only thing that can see the aura? In other words, if you can see an aura then if you close your eye or put an obstacle over it, is the aura still visible to you or does it have to be transmitted to the physical eye?

AW: No, you see it with the spiritual eye.

Q: But if you blank out the eyes physically so light doesn't get in, can you still see it?

Olga Worrall: You still see it . . .

AW: A blind man can see auras.

Voice: A blind man?

OW: Yes, they can see it—if they are clairvoyant.

AW: In fact, in England there was a young fellow who was blind. As he grew up he developed the idea that he should be able to see with his spiritual sight. He traveled all over England lecturing and didn't have anyone with him. He visited my home town when he was in his late twenties. While he was standing on the railroad platform waiting for the train, a couple came up to him with a blind man and asked him if he would see that this fellow got on the train properly and got off at the proper station. He said, "Yes, I'll take care of him. I'm blind myself."

Olga, seated beside her husband, does not look much like a woman of psychic gifts and healing powers. Rather her appearance is that of a dark-haired, bright-eyed, extroverted American housewife. Her neighbors know her for her skill in flower growing and her leadership of the community flower club as much as they do for the spiritual healing work she does in a church clinic—and the prayer period she and her husband dedicate each evening to literally thousands who write or telephone for help.

Olga is a woman of remarkable diversity. A charming hostess, a magnificent cook, everything about her home—and her life— seems to be in perfect order. She keeps her world tidy as a pin. Yet she also accepts the spiritual side of her life and its demands as an entirely normal part of her world. The psychic episode, the prophetic impression, the clairvoyant experience—all of this to Olga is part of the busy day:

OW: When I was teaching high school, I had two blind girls in my typing class. One day when I got onto the elevator, the elevator man said to me, "Mrs. Worrall, be as quiet as you can—the two blind girls are coming—and see if they will know whether you are in the elevator." So I went into the corner of the elevator and was quiet as could be. The two girls got onto the elevator and one said to the other, "Mrs. Worrall is here, I can feel her," and the other girl said, "Yes, I can feel her too." Then I spoke up and said, "What did you feel?"

"We felt something that was just you around us. You were giving something to us as you were standing there." Now they were picking up my aura. I said, "Someone else might have been giving it to you. How did you know it was me giving that off?" They said, "Oh, everybody gives off something different. We know."

They were born blind. They could type. They could do everything. They'd go into the room and they certainly had their radar going because they never bumped into a thing. When I first had them in the class I was a little apprehensive. . . . But they didn't touch a thing other than they were supposed to. And the way they handled a typewriter!

The importance of the role played by the Worralls in investigation and exploration of the paranormal both in the United States and abroad has been monumental. Through their writings, lectures, and their healings reaching out freely to thousands, they have helped spur the whole reawakening of psychic concern. The areas explored in their seminars touched in depth virtually every major field of extrasensory phenomena, including psychic photography, materializations, and ectoplasm—as well as scientific aspects and avenues of explanation, fields in which Ambrose Worrall by his own training and career is particularly knowledgeable.

Those who have not investigated or are not familiar with psychic matters may find many of these subjects strange, bewildering, and even wholly unbelievable. Yet to this author and reporter the claims for and against should be explored and discussed. The astral body and astral travel are subjects about which Ambrose not only claims much knowledge but also personal involvement. His personal experiences represent one side of his story. The meaning— the interpretation—is largely objective and questioning. On the one hand, he talks of the experience without explaining or defining it too closely. This is what happened as he knew it. But then come the harder questions: What and why—and how?

As a boy he dreamed one night that he had gone to the home of a girl whom he knew; he dreamed that he was in her room, that he leaned over and spoke to her. He knew that he was not there, that he was still in his bed in his own home; yet he was there, he was certain, in another sense, another dimension.

On the following day he encountered this girl on the street and she demanded, "What were you doing in our house last night, in my room. . . ."

He speaks of this experience as an example of "involuntary astral travel."

This is the man who for many years designed the highly technical details of aircraft. It is also the man who explores electrical and other kinds of force fields as possible explanations for, or sources of, psychic power and experience.

These two people examine and consider everything in their lives; nothing is too difficult or out of style for their attention. But they also question, challenge, and test, as objectively as possible, their own religious and psychic experiences.

Ambrose maintains that the scientific perspective is extremely important in the unfolding story in which religion and the psychic world, as well as science itself, have become sometimes partners, sometimes foes:

AW: There is plenty of evidence of the unwillingness of science to change its own conclusions for new ones and by so doing to bring about revolutionary changes in the world. It was a development of applied mechanics and electrodynamics early in the nineteenth century that changed the world's economy through industrial revolution. Some scientists have occasionally come to premature conclusions and made statements indicating that science had reached or was in sight of the ultimate goal. This was clearly shown near the end of the nineteenth century when many scientists voiced their opinions that essentially everything in the universe could be explained in terms of the principles of mechanics. In the 1890's the president of a national organization of physicists expressed the opinion that all the important basic discoveries in physics had been made and that all that remained to be done was the extension of the precision of measurements . . . get a few more decimal points in there.

Time soon proved that his conclusions were wrong, for within a few years a series of startling discoveries were made, such as radioactivity, X rays, the photoelectric effect, followed by the quantum theory and the theory of relativity, which changed our concepts of the universe in many respects, especially with regard to its size. If such rapid changes can take place in the science of material things, then scientific research into life energies and their relation to health could bring about a revolution in the treatment of disease and the maintenance of health that would have a profound effect upon world economy and improve the lot of millions.

It could be instrumental in the prevention of war and crime which are the outward evidence of sick minds at work. In using the term spiritual healing, for want of a better term, to describe the basic subject of these discussions, we are indicating the effect of unexplored forces upon living matter rather than purely the effect of known agents upon matter in a living body.

As we look at advances in knowledge, we find a definite pattern forming. In a half century of time we have progressed from a purely mechanistic theory to the conclusion that some of the major concepts of science must be revised to meet the conditions imposed by the discovery of the wave nature of the electron and proton. Thus we find that science is at least probing in the area in which spiritual healing forces seem to work.

The ill-informed are prone to believe that only those things that can be seen, felt, or heard are real. This is the case with the majority of the sick that come for treatment. They expect to get something they can see, taste, or feel, for to them this is real and can be expected to have some noticeable effect upon their particular imbalance or ill health.

Many would need instruction in laymen's language before they could accept spiritual healing as they would orthodox methods. We are consciously aware of certain vibrations that affect our physical senses. These vibrations must be multiplied more than a million times to encompass the total spectrum of frequencies known to science. Somewhere in that vest realm of unregistered vibration are the radiations or frequencies that restore health through spiritual healing. The task of science is to discover them, control them, and harness them in the service of man.

Does their willingness to explore all the aspects of psychic research mean that the Worralls accept all psychic claims as valid?

The answer is that they do not. They demand proof and are as exacting in their own self-appraisal and with their own failures as they are with others. The fact that they accept no money from anyone for anything that they do or say in their healing ministry eliminates the possibility of profiting from the sickness or trouble or need of others who come to them.

They condemn, moreover, the heartless frauds committed at times in the name of some cults or religions. Both Ambrose and Olga admit readily that many supposed mediums fraudulently prey on credulity to extract money from those who can least afford it. Regardless of his own psychic episodes and of many manifestations that he and Olga accept as totally valid, Ambrose at the same time declares: "This is not to say that there isn't fraud in some materialization seances. We've seen plenty of it. And we have also seen the genuine. . . ."

They say that around us is a viable and vibrant psychic world that most of us do not know. It is the world of the spirit, the other side of the coin of creation.

In this strange world there are often deeply moving stories, hard to believe yet equally hard not to believe. Olga tells of a woman who came to the New Life Clinic healing, counseling, and prayer service held every Thursday at the Mt. Washington United Methodist Church in Baltimore:

The first time she came she asked me to give her healing because she was suffering from varicose veins, under the knees. The doctor and patient were hesitant about the idea of stripping the veins. . . . I placed my hands on the area involved and the condition began to improve. Several weeks later she came to the Clinic before the service started and asked to speak with me. She said, "Mrs. Worrall, I want to thank you so much for what the New Life Clinic is doing for me." She continued, "I was literally led to get your book from the library. I went to the library with my son to find books for him but with no intention of getting a book for myself, and I actually felt as if someone pushed me in front of this bookcase and there was your book. It has meant a great deal to me."

While she was telling me this I saw build up next to her the spirit of a woman of dignity and culture, who told me that she was the girl's grandmother and that she had need of her granddaughter's forgiveness. She then proceeded to tell me that she had been very possessive of the girl's mother and she hated the granddaughter because she had taken up so much of her daughter's time; she had been a very vindictive woman, a miserable person while on earth, according to what she was telling me. She said, "I must have my granddaughter's forgiveness. I cannot go on this way."

I gave the message to the granddaughter and she said, "Why, Mrs. Worrall," and began to cry, and asked me to ask the grandmother to give more information about the relationship in the household between herself and the granddaughter. She then said, "Everything that you have said is right." I said, "You know, your grandmother did love you but she didn't know how to tell you because she was so jealous, but in her heart she really cared for you." I said, "She wants your forgiveness because it will help her to grow spiritually." She said, "Oh, I do forgive my grandmother." She was crying and I left her, until she could compose herself. I went on into the sanctuary where the healing services are held.

On the 10th of February, she wrote this letter:

Dear, dear Mrs. Worrall:
What a wonderful gift I received through you. Through your message from my Grandmother last Thursday—in one flash, in one moment, God performed the most fabulous piece of surgery!
    The moment grandmother asked for forgiveness, I forgave! Years of hard feelings and harsh thoughts were erased. I feel like a malignancy in my soul has been removed. After realizing the full implications of it, I not only was able to forgive *her*—but also the bruising and painful memories of my troubled and bitter childhood in Nazi Germany are lifted. I imagine, when one forgives under God's guidance the forgiving is total;—Yes, I even forgave myself for the things I have done in my life, which I wasn't particularly proud of!—Now, I think all the clogging waste matter is removed and I can be a better functioning channel. How strongly and firmly I have been guided this last year! It's been a hard struggle, but it surely has been worth it! I was literally pushed onto your book and into your arms.
    I have already thanked the good Lord—now all that's left is to thank you, and I do this most lovingly and sincerely.
                                                    (signed) S. M. D.

This young lady is a member of a Jewish congregation in Baltimore.

The possibility that our age of science will uncover hitherto unrecognized forces, energies, and truths about our universe and ourselves creates the great potential of wider understanding, perhaps of new spiritual elevation for all people of this earth.

In this new beginning, this quest, the average individual often thinks first of the gifted, the seer, the prophet, the clairvoyant.

Who then are counted among the gifted? Is not the answer perhaps—all of us? Are not such gifts a matter of learning, of understanding, and of reaching out?

2
You the Clairvoyant

In a suburban community in northern Westchester County in New York, two next-door neighbors vied with each other regarding the progress of their offspring. When the mother of one bought a violin for her six-year-old daughter, the other mother bought an equally expensive violin for her seven-year-old son. Unfortunately, the boy couldn't be driven to the violin and after a few bleak lessons flatly refused to have anything more to do with it—a decision in which his teacher fully concurred.

The little girl, on the other hand, loved the violin like a living thing; practice to her was the one thing that mattered. Within a year, her gift was apparent to all who heard her efforts; here was a violinist.

From what source comes this kind of gift? The answer often is impossible to determine, particularly when, as here, neither child had any immediate forebears with any distinction whatsoever in music. Genetics, despite much scientific investigation, still has no definitive answers on this point.

This story of the gifted and nongifted child mirrors exactly the situation in clairvoyance, which also is a talent, a gift of the spirit, more developed in some than in others, and again for reasons hard to explore or understand. Certainly the two major participants in the seminars appear to be extremely gifted seers. Ambrose's family had some very slight psychic interest; some of them attended spiritualist services, and Ambrose's father may have had some gift in extrasensory areas. Olga's background had little in that direction; her family were Russian and Hungarian and members of the Russian Orthodox Church. Ambrose, along with his gift of seeing and hearing at the spiritual level, was also mechanically gifted. Olga was a normal child in all respects except for the things she "saw," predictions of things that would happen, words that came to her which she would say spontaneously, not even knowing why she did this.

Clairvoyance means "clear seeing." More exactly, perhaps, it could be called enlightened seeing, seeing beyond the clouded vision of physical optics, seeing that reaches to other, higher levels, to nondimensional and nontemporal planes.

There is evidence that the talent of clairvoyance, however great or small, exists in virtually every human being, that the impulse— the vision unbidden in the mind, the dream—springs up from time to time within all of us.

It is possible to develop this force in some measure, to learn to respond to it, to practice a little on what might be called our spiritual violin strings. But before one can even begin such an approach, it is important to grasp the meaning, the significance of this gift.

To become the clairvoyant, one must first realize that this is a power not to be treated lightly or wrongly. There are many times when the clairvoyant moment comes to us. It comes unbidden, unexpected, often unrecognized and ignored. It is a sudden glimpse of tomorrow; it is a premonition that we must not go in here— or that we must. It is a voice speaking where none is actually heard. It is a warning. It is a promise.

The clairvoyant gift may be small or great in each of us; it can, however, be developed. It can be tried, tested, recognized, used. But it is not a childish toy or a cocktail-hour sideshow.

It is extremely difficult to express or describe the metaphysical in terms of the physical. Clairvoyants often find their words inadequate to translate what they actually experience.

At one early stage in the seminars, Dr. Laidlaw, in response to a statement Olga made in attempting to describe the nature of the ethereal body, declared, "What you are saying, Olga, implies that in addition to there being a spiritual eye as well as a physical eye, the other senses also have spiritual components?"

OW: That is correct. In the spirit world you can see, hear, smell, taste, and touch. I believe that a clairvoyant has some unusual mechanism that permits him to respond more readily to spiritual impressions while in the physical body than someone not so gifted.

Voice: Could we jump right to the very next step in this discussion? I think we know each other well enough that I can speak frankly about your spirit guides. So here we have guides who aren't burdened with physical bodies. . . . But from the hard evidence I've had, certain information you receive does come through the guides. They do get through your spiritual body into your physical body to the extent that you articulate their information verbally.

AW: Right.

Voice: So from the evidence you present in action you have the possibility of a spiritual entity devoid of a body interacting through you. And the information comes into the physical domain. . . .

Dr. Laidlaw: But with a spiritual body, however, isn't it? I mean, which is not formless. It is the spiritual body interacting. . . .

AW: Yes, it has the same form that this body has.

Voice: It has form, therefore. . . .

OW: The spiritual body has form.

Question: And I suppose that the kind of guides that we're dealing with in your case are also dimensional?

OW: As they appear to us they are three-dimensional.

AW: They are dimensional but they are not of the density of physical matter. Material things pass through these forms, just like I put my hand through the air. The air is there and I feel it but I do not see it.

OW: While we've been sitting here this afternoon, Dr. Gardner's mother has been standing by his side. Your mother is in the other world, Dr. Gardner.

Dr. William Gardner:[1] Yes.

OW: You resemble your mother. She has been asking me to tell you that she is with you.

Dr. Gardner: Well, I thank you.

OW: She tells me you took after her side of the family. Now, you see, she's just as real to me. . . .

Dr. Gardner: Is she aware of what you're saying?

OW: Oh yes, because when you sat down she appeared to me and she's been standing there all this time, very much interested in what's been going on. I would call her psychic; when she was on earth she was very intuitive and very much interested in these things, whether you knew this or not. She is very happy that you are here, and was listening to our conversation. She was so anxious to have me tell you that she was with you, but I hesitated at first to convey this information to you because I didn't know just how you would take it.

Dr. Gardner: Well, I take it . . . all in the family. I thank you.

OW: Good! She is a very, very sweet person.

Voice: You see, that's what's frustrating. I can't see Dr. Gardner's mother, and why?

OW: No, you can't see her, but I can see her . . . and why can't you?

AW: I had a fellow work for me one time who was an engineer and he had 20-20 vision. He flew an airplane. He had wonderful eyesight, but he couldn't see any colors. He used a red pencil to show a debit on the sheet and he had to put a circle around it; he couldn't see it was red. He couldn't believe that I could see magenta and yellow and violet and all these different colors.

Voice: I guess that's as good an example as any of what I'm talking about.

Dr. Gardner: Olga, when you used the word "seeing" in connection with my mother, can you amplify that a bit for my understanding? Tell us exactly what you mean by using the word "seeing," like seeing this piece of paper.

OW: Well, to me it is like seeing this piece of paper, but. . . .

Dr. Gardner: There must be some difference.

1. Doctor of medicine; internist in private practice in New York City.

OW: There is this difference because I know she's a spirit, you see, and I saw her through my forehead.

Dr. Gardner: Does she have dimensions?

OW: She has dimensions. She's just as dimensional as you are.

Dr. Gardner: If you had a mirror here, would there be an image?

OW: No, there wouldn't be an image because she was not materialized. Her spiritual body would not reflect in a mirror, but if she had clothed herself with physical particles she would then have been seen because the materialized form would reflect light. If someone in this room had the power of materializing spirits, and such materialization was accomplished, then all of us would have been able to see your mother.

Dr. Gardner: Is she here now?

OW: No, she has faded away from my sight now. I'm not clairvoyant at this moment, but momentarily I was clairvoyant and each time I would look her way my clairvoyance would come into play and I would see her standing there. I don't see her now.

Dr. Gardner: Will you describe her appearance?

OW: She was not a tall woman. Her head came just a wee bit higher than your head as she stood beside your chair and she was about my build as she appeared to me, but her face and your face were so similar. . . .

Dr. Laidlaw: Did you know that she was Bill's mother or did you assume it?

OW: No, no, she told me! "I'm his mother."

Dr. Laidlaw: You heard this clairaudiently. . . .

OW: She said, "I'm his mother. Tell him I'm with him."

Dr. Gardner: That's interesting. Once long ago. . . . What was the name of that previous house where the Society for Psychical Research used to meet—way downtown?

Dr. Laidlaw: In their former quarters? The Hyslop House.

Dr. Gardner: They had a seance there—in darkness. When it came my turn she simply said, "It's mother." In those days she was living and I found that difficult. . . .

OW: Your mother is in the spirit world now. . . . I knew it was your mother that I saw and that she was in the other life. Some clairvoyants can turn their gifts on at will, but mine is spontaneous; I could never say that I am going to become clairvoyant at a given time and give you a message. I couldn't do that, it manifests when there is a need.

Dr. Gardner: Why wouldn't she say anything to me?

OW: Because you wouldn't hear her. Unless you have the gift of clairaudience you could not hear her, because when she speaks in this manner she creates no sound waves that would register on the physical hearing apparatus.

Dr. Gardner: Why not?

OW: I don't know. However, it appears that the transmission is by thought waves instead of by sound waves.

This case of Dr. Gardner's mother reveals three problems involved in the clairvoyant life. Is it ever possible for the clairvoyant to transmit totally what is happening? Is the apparent episode a valid experience? Can it be tested empirically?

To find the answers, particularly in relating the whole subject with the usually more mundane and solid-matter world of the layman, one could best start by increasing his own understanding of the scope of these experiences.

Olga, for example, reported another case in that particular seminar session. It is interesting to note the easy flow of the story and of the details, particularly since Olga simply had no way of knowing in advance anything about this child who—by normal lights—was not there at all:

During the summer months, occasionally traveling ministers going to Washington, D.C., stop by at the New Life Clinic. About a year ago two such ministers with their wives and children attended the New Life Clinic service. I saw five children as I stood in the pulpit (I was preaching that Thursday). One little girl in particular attracted my attention. She appeared to be about seven or eight years old. She wore a huge bow in her hair—quite old-fashioned, I thought. After the service was over, the children ran out to play, and I saw this little girl playing with the other four children. The parents asked if I would have lunch with them and I suggested we could all go someplace to eat. They said, "That won't be necessary, we have our trailer . . . and we'll have sandwiches. . . ."

So we all piled into the rear end of this little trailer truck—it was a cute thing—and four children joined us. I asked, "Where is the fifth one?" They said, "What do you mean the fifth one?" I said, "Why, the fifth child you had in church with you today." The parents looked at me and said, "Why, we each have just two children." So I described the little girl; I said that she was playing right out there. One of the couple's daughters, seven years old, spoke up and said, "Oh yes, that was Margaret." They looked at her with unbelief, then she added, "Margaret comes with us all the time. She's my best friend." She knew this little girl and was in full agreement that I saw Margaret.

Her mother asked, "Where did Margaret go?" The child answered, "When Margaret has to go away, she disappears." Then they began to question the child, "How long have you known Margaret?" And the child said, "Oh, I've known her a long time. She always comes to me when I go to sleep at night." I'll tell you I was shaken because, to me, Margaret was just as real as that little girl who sees Margaret and knows her as her best friend.

The range of clairvoyance is wide. It includes the ability to practice psychometry—the obtaining of information through some object that sends off psychic radiation. Through these radiations, the medium holding the object knows—or sees—past or present associations of the object. Clairvoyance also includes the ability to predict the seemingly unpredictable, to know what has happened and what will happen, to see what cannot be seen. Clairvoyance is a free camera loose in the universe.

Perhaps the truth is that the psychic senses, while duplicated in certain ways at other levels of existence, are not in fact the same as the physical, just as the flash of light in the diamond is not in fact the diamond itself. Does the experience come at the psychic level as a flash of light comes, out of and part of the physical yet of a different kind—a kind against which the laboratory, the test tube, the chemical formula, have thus far shown scant apparent authority?

Eileen Garrett, founder of the magazine *Tomorrow,* has long been accepted as one of the greatest of clairvoyants and healers of the twentieth century. Dr. Laidlaw, as a psychiatrist and student of the paranormal, has held her in the highest regard for her gifts, honesty, and sincerity of purpose.

Consider this following brief sidelight involving Mrs. Garrett and Dr. Laidlaw:

AW: Does anyone want to say anything about psychometry?

Dr. Laidlaw: The question was raised as to whether a name would suffice to psychometrize. Even without a name . . . the first time I met Eileen Garrett, after some discussion about herself, I said to her, "I wonder without my giving you any leads at all, if you can tell me about the most difficult psychiatric problem that I'm working with currently."

She said, "Yes, I can," and she went on to give me a detailed case history. The interesting thing was that it was a case I instantly recognized as being in my current practice but it wasn't the one that I was thinking of. But, as she went on, I realized that actually this was a more difficult case than the one that I had just spontaneously picked out. After she had given me many very detailed facts and a dynamic interpretation of this case, she then smiled and said to me, "Now, I'll tell you about the case that you had in mind." She then proceeded to do so with the same psychological insight and accuracy of detail.

Carlton Sherwood:[2] I remember some years ago being in London. Eileen Garrett was there at the same time and, with another friend, we drove way up the Thames for lunch. The building was a beautiful old restaurant. We were just visiting . . . and enjoying the day, and I pulled out a tobacco pouch at the close of the lunch, filled my pipe and closed the pouch. All of a sudden just by impulse I handed the pouch to Eileen and said, "Psychometrize that for me, will you?" She took it. While sitting there at the lunch table, she told me almost everything

2. Businessman; trustee, American Society for Psychical Research.

about its background. It was a leather tobacco pouch that had belonged to my brother. Two years before he had been killed in an automobile accident; his car went into the Niagara River. And she told me who it was and a large part of the details of what happened, just casually like that.

Eileen Garrett typifies one aspect of those greatly endowed with the spiritual gifts: they are able to use many avenues of the psychic forces. They have the gift of second sight, of clairaudience; they look seemingly beyond the borders of earth time.

Each case, to the clairvoyant, the psychically gifted, is unique. Each presents its own challenge to the individual who must try to find out what is happening, what is going wrong, what forces are at work.

Often such forces are deceptive. Often they involve, literally, issues of life and death:

OW: One case in particular comes to mind, that of a college girl who at the age of about ten or eleven suddenly began to write reams of poetry about the blessed mother and Jesus; most unusual for a member of a Protestant church. This went on for about ten years. The girl never wanted to go out to play; all she wanted to do was write poetry. Soon after she graduated from college with honors, she tried to commit suicide. She was in the hospital when we were called in on the case. . . .

AW: This girl was twenty-one years old, a very pretty girl. The physicians thought that by medication and treatment they could bring her out of her psychotic state, but they were not successful. Finally they informed her parents that she would have to be placed in an institution. The girl's mother discussed the situation with a friend of ours who in turn called us for help. I suggested that she obtain a photograph of the girl and bring it with her to our home. She brought a photograph of the girl as she appeared in her graduation cap and gown. As I held the photograph in my hand, I became aware of a number of people on the other side of life. They gave me their names, aunt this and uncle that, and so on. The friend said, "Yes, they are relatives of this girl." I said, "Well, they are interested, but they haven't the faintest idea what to do and neither do I." I said, "We have to find somebody who knows what to do." Almost immediately this group of spirit people started to recede and they went up somewhere—they felt to me as though they were about 50 feet above my head—and then another group joined the relatives, and they were all talking. It was as if I had two radio stations on at the same time. I couldn't tell what they were saying, but they didn't talk very long.

Then the first group was completely eliminated from my consciousness. One member of the second group detached himself, like an airplane out of the group diving down on the target, and came down and said, "Don't do anything about this until we come back. We're going to the hospital." The episode was terminated, shut off—just like you'd switch off a light. I decided we'd just have to wait for further developments. We sat around and talked for about a half hour. Then a voice spoke to me and said, "All of you go into the healing room[3] and take the photograph along with you." "Well," I said, "I've got the word. Let's go upstairs."

We sat in the healing room. I had the photograph in my hand when suddenly the picture started to vibrate. I thought my hand was shaking and I became a little concerned about it; immediately there appeared before me a man who said, "You're worried about the photograph shaking?" I said, "Yes." He said, "Don't worry about it. I'll explain it to you. My name is Dr. Thornton. I'm a specialist in mental cases, and we have connected this room by means of a psychic tube with the room in the hospital occupied by the girl. This room has very high frequencies . . . there are much lower frequencies around the girl. Through this tube we are feeding the high frequency from this room to the hospital room and when the frequency around the girl is brought up to the same level as in this room she will be cured; she is possessed by an entity and this entity will not be able to tolerate the higher frequency and will have to leave the girl."

And I . . . the old critical mind comes in . . . asked Dr. Thornton, "What hospital is she in?" (I didn't know what hospital she was in.) And he gave the name of the hospital. I said, "What floor is she on?"

3. The room in the Worrall home where patients are treated and where the Worralls sit in healing prayer every evening at 9:00 P.M.

He said she was on the second floor. So I turned to the friend who had called us and asked, "Is this girl on the second floor of the hospital?" She replied, "Yes."

Dr. Laidlaw: She was not able to hear this voice?

AW: No one present heard it but myself.

I said to Olga and the friend, "They must have the right girl." Dr. Thornton said, "Don't worry about the photograph shaking," and he disappeared. I became very interested in the vibrating photograph and wanted to see what the outcome would be. The amplitude of the motion got less and less but the frequency got faster and faster until it disappeared altogether. In trying to explain what happened I concluded that something connected with the girl, some emanation from her, seemed to be impressed on the photograph. What I registered in the beginning was a slow pulsation of the photograph corresponding to the girl's low rate of frequency, and as it became faster and faster during her treatment, it indicated the effect of this high frequency being fed to her through the astral tube and that the frequency around her was increasing. Finally, the frequencies in the two rooms became equal and the vibrating of the photograph ceased. Soon thereafter, Dr. Thornton appeared again and said, "You can tell the lady to go home, the girl is cured. I've left one of my assistants to take care of her and she will have no more trouble. I have to go on another case so you'll have to excuse me. Good night." And he was gone.

I relayed his message to our friend . . . it must have been about ten o'clock at night by this time. She went home. At six o'clock the following morning she was awakened by the ringing of the telephone. It was the girl, calling her from the hospital. She said, "I've just been discharged from the hospital, but for some reason I can't go to my home. May I go to your home on the island?" Our friend said, "Why, certainly, you go down to the boat and I'll meet you there." Our friend took the girl to her home on the island where they stayed for a number of weeks. The girl recovered completely and had no recurrence of the problem thereafter.

This experience impressed me by the matter-of-fact way it happened. I mean, it was as if it were the people here, like we are, discussing something and saying, "Well, we'll try something." They tried it and it worked, and they came back to say, "It's all right, it's all over."

Q: Is this a fairly common mechanism, this business of changing a person's frequency?

AW: Never heard of it before nor since. . . .

It does appear that the mechanisms—if such there are—by which clairvoyant episodes occur are little understood. Although the gifted ones know that the gift can be developed, strengthened, sought for, they themselves often cannot explain in any realistic sense how communication at the psychic level occurs. Ambrose calls it a creative force and describes it as wave energy. Yet in listening to the dialogue and interchanges of the seminar, we realize that much of what occurs is beyond the experience of most of us:

Dr. Henry K. Puharich:[4] Earlier you mentioned the silver cord and, at the beginning of the afternoon, reference was made to the electromagnetic field around inanimate objects and memory storage from them as evidenced by psychometry, and again with the whole time situation, two incidents come to mind: One happened a rather long time ago with the famed mystic Edgar Cayce; when he was about to step into an elevator and suddenly saw something strange. It was dark in the elevator and he realized that none of these people had any auras. He stepped back out of the elevator, which fell a few moments later and all these people were killed.

The second recent incident was the following: I happened to have occasion to be with Peter Hurkos, the Dutch psychic, this past fall when he related an incident which occurred last summer. He was called out to Vietnam to ascertain whether a certain man had been actually captured, was alive or dead, etc. And while he was stopping over at (I forget which airport it was but it was in the Far East) there was a reporter near him (the news had leaked out that he was going there) and he looked out on the airfield toward a large plane and, in his way of expressing it, he said, "That plane is dead." He told the reporter that he saw it as black. The reporter said, "What do you mean?"

4. Doctor of medicine; author of *Sacred Mushroom* and *Beyond Telepathy* (Garden City, N.Y.: Doubleday & Company, 1959 and 1962 respectively); Director of Medical Research, Intelectron Corporation.

and he just said, "It's dead." A few hours later the plane did crash and all aboard were killed.

Now, do you have any explanation for situations like this?

AW: These things are very difficult to explain, but evidently the mechanism for the crash of the plane was already set in motion in the creative cycle, and there was no way to prevent it from being brought out to the conclusion in sequential time, and by his psychic gifts Hurkos was able to see this.

Dr. Puharich: Was the plane, though, sending out some kind of radiation to tell him that or he just projecting it onto the plane by tuning into "whole time"?

AW: There again you have the problem to decide just which way this works. We don't know which way it works. All we know is that you have an experience and you try to explain it and you don't come up with the answer because you don't know the mechanism.

Voice: Doesn't that touch on a very delicate philosophical aspect? If all the events are laid out and concluded there in "whole time" then the entire discussion earlier regarding evil forces vs. forces of good has no point. . . . It seems to me if it's all there already it really makes no difference what our approach is.

AW: You get into predestination. It is very difficult to fit all these things together. It's like—why did God create the mosquitoes to bite the human being and give him trouble? There are millions of questions but no answers, and this conception of time is just a way to try to explain things that happen, like getting a complete symphony in a flash or the clairvoyant receiving the complete story in a flash, as has happened to me many times.

OW: But something can be done. . . . If someone in charge of that plane could have been approached by Peter (of course they wouldn't necessarily listen to Peter), and he could have said, "Ground that plane because there is something wrong with it," he could have prevented that plane leaving for that unfortunate crash. But we know there are few people that would heed a warning of this nature and they could have had Peter arrested for creating a disturbance if he could not have pinpointed the trouble. So, when you see these things you are utterly helpless because people won't believe. I'm sure Peter Hurkos has had a lot of problems in that way.

When Edgar Cayce saw darkness in that elevator—apparently there was some mechanical trouble with it that they had not detected and it was because of this mechanism being out of commission that it had to crash. You see, if Edgar Cayce had said, "Everybody get out of that elevator because there's going to be trouble, it's not working properly," they would probably have paid no attention to him. They would have said the man was out of his mind.

Voice: That happened with a man I know who had precognitive dreams and when they were related they always came true, and he got into trouble with the authorities.

OW: When you're psychic you have to be very careful that you're with the right people because they can easily say, "What did you do?" or "What ulterior motive did you have?" So psychics learn to keep their mouths shut, even though they see things happen, because nine times out of ten they can't do anything about it. But if you're with the right people and see things. . . . They say, "Coming events cast their shadows before," and if they listen perhaps they can avoid a catastrophe.

Where then does the information, the clairvoyant warning or direction, come from? Ambrose and Olga, basically psychic healers, who have done this work over many years for the benefit of others, believe it comes virtually as an answer to the patient's inner need.

OW: Ambrose says that often in giving spiritual healing he will receive instructions or guidance that could be very helpful to the patient. . . .

Q: Where do you think that comes from?

AW: It comes from the need of the individual concerned. You see, when a person has a need, he is sending out signals for help into what has been referred to as the Universal Mind. The Universal Mind responds to the signals and if the response can find a channel through which it can pass it will be transmitted to the one in need. Now this is all theory. I can't prove any of it, but it satisfies my type of reasoning.

Voice: You would call it the Universal Mind. Olga, before, you said that you have discarnates—physicians, etc.—who were helping you. Is that what you mean by . . . ?

OW: Yes, they can be used as channels for signals from the Universal Mind.

AW: I get information both ways. Often I get it direct—at least I can't sense that it's coming from a discarnate. . . .

Q: You sense it telepathically or hear it?

AW: It comes all ways: I get it telepathically—I have heard voices; I have known when it came from an individual, and also, I have been able to detect if it came from the Universal Mind. In other words, I know when it comes from this strange silence and I satisfy my questioning mind by saying it comes out of the Universal Mind that knows all things; that the need of the patient is sending a signal out and that I just happen to be available and properly attuned so that the reply to that signal, that radar if you want to call it that, reflects it back through me to the patient. Now, if the information is of a very personal nature I won't be able to recall what was transmitted through me.

OW: You can get messages of such a personal nature that it would be absolutely wrong to even let anyone else know, and when a message such as this comes through it has a unique way of just flowing through me and then it fades out of my consciousness because it doesn't belong to me. And, of course, you don't want to clutter up your mind with everything you get. You might like to know that I hear clairaudiently through the top of my head and I see clairvoyantly through my forehead.

Q: You really can't remember it, or you just shut it off?

OW: I don't shut it off, I just am unable to recall it. You doctors might like to know that when I'm in a strong state of clairvoyance I feel dull at the base of my head—I feel as if everything has been blocked off in that area, but everything is stimulated in the area at the top of my head. . . . I've wondered ever since I was a child why, when receiving clairvoyance, that I felt numb in this area—yet the top of my head was unusually stimulated.

Dr. Karlis Osis:[5] Would you please describe the areas with your hand clearly so there is no mistake. It's very important.

OW: It's the back of my head. . . .

5. Doctor of philosophy; Director of Research, American Society for Psychical Research.

In sum, then, what is this force of which they speak?

Ambrose and Olga believe that it is the force of God, the creative force that is within each of us, dormant and unrecognized and unused in most of us, yet there.

To attain the fullest use of these forces requires understanding that unfolds only with actual practice and development of knowledge in areas that reach beyond the normal range of experience.

Near the close of one of the early sessions, Ambrose sought to describe his own idea of the nature of these forces within us and with which we live and work and strive in both the psychic and physical sense:

AW: The image is not the aura . . . let me explain this. The image of God in man is spirit—you wouldn't see *that* light. Or, let me put it this way, if you were capable of actually seeing it you would be absorbed into it. When we talk of seeing the image of God in man we mean that we see God's characteristics reflected in man. Man is using the divine principle of creation when he thinks; he is creating. The first step in creation is thinking and it goes out in wave form and affects his aura. That gives the aura its color.

Voice: You mentioned the computerized aspect. . . .

AW: The mind is a computer. It takes thoughts and ideas that come into it and puts them together into a form, which can be willed into manifestation.

Voice: But I guess it's impossible to think without doing something in the nondimensional . . . we don't know the boundary line . . .

AW: There is no boundary line. The image of God is where everything starts and all creation is from that image: the body itself, the spiritual body, everything is a creation from that which we can't describe and which has no dimensions. All creation is in wave form. . . .

Vague. Difficult. Elusive.

There is much one can learn from the greatly gifted, the masters. But each of us who seeks this road must ultimately find and follow its path alone, in his or her own terms, at his or her own levels.

3
An Aura of Gold

The colors of auras, say the metaphysicians, reflect the individual, what he thinks and believes, what he is.

Dark colors, murky colors, reflect darkness and murkiness of mind, body, or soul; clear, bright colors reflect the brighter aspect of the individual; warm colors speak of an emanating warmth; the golden aura is the aura of the gifted, the pure of heart.

It is a strange, beautiful, and important area of metaphysics, this emanation of soul energy and force and direction. Yet at the same time, perhaps no field in modern parapsychology presents such difficulties as this one, in understanding, in interpretation, and explanation.

To Ambrose, the scientist, the student of modern electronics and force fields—and the sensitive in other parapsychological areas—the answers here evolve out of the spiritual-physical universe, acting and interacting, one side upon the other.

In his own informal, yet curiously exact words, Ambrose outlined to the seminar what he knows scientifically, intuitively, empirically, regarding the aura—and what he sees:

I have never seen an aura around a dead body, so I can only assume that when the spirit leaves the body the emanation, the aura, goes with the spirit, the spirit being in the spiritual body which St. Paul mentioned in the Bible when he said that we have a spiritual body and a natural body. To me they are both natural but one is in the physical realm and one is in the spiritual realm. Now the aura portrays many things and, to me, it tells me first the type of person, whether he is outgoing, generous. It tells me: "I have something that I must give to the world." This is the large aura. Then there is the one that says: "I'm going to get everything I can out of the world." This is the tight aura, drawn in. So you have these two extremes and everything in between, of course.

Auric emanations apparently have frequencies comparable to the light spectrum but on an entirely different octave. Those that are of the earth, earthy, will have the denser colors. Those that are of the spiritual nature will have light, pastel shades of color. To me . . . I explain these to myself by saying that these are differences in frequencies. When I see the whole aura colored gray I know the person is despondent, depressed. If I see red splotches in the aura, this can indicate anger or fear. Browns and greens in the aura indicate things of the earth. Perhaps the person is a horticulturist and likes things that grow. If I see a deep gold color around the head, he is an intellectual but more interested in things of a material nature. If I see this in a light lemon color, he is interested in things of a spiritual nature. You can even see black in some persons' auras. This is a deep form of hate or destruction, and it could be fear which is very close to hate. I don't very often see black in auras but I often see red. I've seen a very dark purple aura around a person who is extremely religious but so narrow that he believes everybody is on the wrong path except himself. They are good persons . . . but very unenlightened spiritually. . . .

Ambrose also pinpointed specifically the physical-psychical relationship of the aura as he understands and interprets it:

The aura is with the spiritual body and when the spiritual body occupies the physical body the aura is seen around the latter because the spiritual body inhabits it at that particular time. This auric emanation is part of the spiritual body; there appears to be no auric emanation from the dead; but I have seen spiritual entities with beautiful auras around them. The aura goes with the spirit and I believe, too, that it is a creation from the image of God and that the mind of the person influences the aura by the selection of ideas entertained. This colors the aura.

In a pure state the aura would be just like white light, as it is around the heads of the saints, who have purified themselves. They have put their "selves" out of the way so that the image of God expresses itself through them in white light.

"Seeing" the aura is in no sense an optical function of the physical eye. Both Ambrose and Olga maintain that one "sees" the aura— "senses" might be a better word—with the spiritual eye and quite spontaneously. Thus it is possible for blind people to be aware of auras and for normally sighted people to "see" them when their eyes are closed. Olga insists that she "sees" the aura through the center of her forehead.

But every living being, human or animal, radiates an aura, say the Worralls, and if this radiation is itself a life form, as many claim, the question comes: Why do some persons see these auras clearly and others cannot see them at all? On this point Dr. Henry K. Puharich commented:

The reason some people see auras and others don't is that the tissues of the body are very peculiar. You can pass microwaves through some people's hands and they will neatly polarize the radar waves. Other people don't, so that we may have polarization elements of the eye in some people. All it takes is a few degrees of polarization to get a unique effect.

Polarization of the vision would be, if the theory were demonstrated to be true, one example of psychic force directly affecting physical vision. The polarization would be in effect a changing of the focus of the eye to see the unseeable out of another plane of reality.

However, we must bear in mind that all of this is only theory. There are, in fact, many theories regarding auric emanations because so much remains unknown. Why do some people see auras all the time, and others only when their gift appears to be unusually strong or conditions appear unusually suited to psychic action and reaction?

Answers are still not established on any sound scientific basis. Investigation appears to be still in the explorative state. And even the most gifted individuals sometimes find it difficult to describe what is happening, to cross the bridge verbally from one plane to the other.

Ambrose, one of the most gifted in articulating his own psychic experiences, related an experience in Baltimore—at a gathering in which someone raised the question of why auras change in color and intensity. Ambrose led this discussion. One of the participants was the headmaster of a local school. The headmaster asked Ambrose how often he saw auras:

AW: I said that I see them occasionally. He asked, "Well, can you tell what people are thinking about when you see the aura?" And I replied, "I can tell the type of thought they are thinking when I see their aura." He said, "Well, can you see anybody's aura now?" I said, "Yes, I can see yours." He said, "Well, I'm going to change it."

So he put his head down for awhile and concentrated. And I saw the whole aura change to a pale blue color. I said, "I know what kind of thought you're thinking. You are thinking a very religious thought because your whole aura turned into a pale blue color which, to me, means a religious type of thought." He said, "Well, I've got to admit that I was saying over and over in my mind a prayer my mother taught me when I was a little boy. But I'm going to change it again now." He put his head down again and in a moment I saw the aura change color. I said, "I'll tell you what you're thinking about now. You are thinking about something which has to do with the earth but on a highly intellectual level. It is a scientific thinking about earth." He just shook his head and said, "A friend of mine is doing research work in the Gobi Desert. I just had a meeting with him about his findings, and I was going over in my mind all that we discussed about his findings in the Gobi Desert. How did you know that?"

I said, "First of all, I saw brown come into your aura right across the lower part of your body, then in the upper part of your body it was green and then up above your head it became a deep gold color. The brown and green have to do with things of the earth. The deep gold color has to do with materialistic type of intellect. So I knew it was an intellectual thought about things of the earth. I couldn't tell it was in the Gobi Desert—but the type of thinking was shown on the aura."

If we could develop a means of detecting auras by instrumentation, then when someone comes into your office you could turn this on and you may find an aura all full of red blotches . . .

Dr. Laidlaw: I think this has great potential. . . .

AW: Yes, if you see an aura full of red blotches you know the fellow is full of anger!

We had a study group back in Cleveland before I was married, and we did all kinds of experiments. Of course we had no instruments, just human beings.

One day one of the members, as he entered the room to attend a meeting, emanated an aura spotted with red dots. As I greeted him, I said, "What made you so angry today?" He said, "What do you mean?" I said, "Something made you angry. You're still carrying it around with you." "Well," he said, "when we quit work I went to my locker to get my soap and my soap was gone, so I went over to where the fellows were washing and there was a man using my soap. I accused him of stealing my soap, and he said it wasn't my soap and I got in a big argument with him."

He carried that anger with him. That was about eight o'clock at night and he had quit work at four o'clock in the afternoon, and he still had the red dots in his aura. That was his anger showing—like a red flag.

As the dialogue on auras expanded, it became clear that to Ambrose the physical as well as the spiritual aspects of auric emanations are equally significant:

AW: A spectroscope reveals the various colors emitted by different elements. Every chemical element known has a distinctive spectrum of its own. The colors of the individual spectrum, the green of magnesium, the red of hydrogen, the violet of calcium, and the yellow of table salt, may give us a clue to the frequencies of healing rays necessary to affect these elements when necessary to restore a diseased organ. Suppose you have a diabetic and he needs a little insulin, could we get the proper kind of ray, the proper kind of frequency that would stimulate the generation of insulin in the body?

We've examined and discussed auras quite a bit in our talks. Healing rays, to be effective, must penetrate the human aura. Now the human aura is dynamic; the colors fluctuate and change. They may be tranquil as still water or impulsive like the flames of a fire. They will reveal peace or turbulence of mind. Some colors will be soft and misty, others appear hard and clear. Some have poorly defined shapes like clouds. Other colors appear as rods, coils, or cones. It has been said that the aura is an index to man's inherent qualities. It may also be a factor in his ability to receive healing rays. In other words, the aura may act as a filter and filter some of the healing rays out or dilute them. . . . If auric colors change the colors of the healing rays as they pass through the physical body, their effectiveness could be reduced or their frequencies modified to such an extent that they would not perform their function.

Psychological or psychiatric treatment could condition a patient's aura and make possible the reception of healing rays which otherwise could not penetrate the colors and turbulence in the aura before such treatments; a tranquilizer may also have a similar effect. So it may be possible that here we have the combination of the psychiatrist and the spiritual healer necessary in order to get results through spiritual healing. . . .

Dr. Laidlaw (to John Pierrakos[1]): Is it true, Dr. Pierrakos, that you are able to see the aura in considerable detail yourself?

Dr. Pierrakos: Yes, but not always in detail. It depends on the conditions. But I see the main characteristics of the aura or the field, and I am able to perceive the pulsatory movement, how many times it pulsates, how many layers there are, the structure of the field, the color in a general overall way, and some of the brightness and interruptions in the field—where there are interruptions in the body.

I am interested in this because I have observed through experience that there is always a relationship between the nature of the field, the aura, and the nature of the person—the type of character structure and

1. Doctor of Medicine; psychiatrist; director, Institute for Bio-energetic Analysis.

the type of illness. For instance, the schizophrenic person has the kind of field which is not the same as that of a neurotic person. Then there is the person who has psychosomatic disturbances in a specific area. The field shows distinct changes. I am interested in that, so I observe the variations of the field and then try to use my psychiatric knowledge or my psychosomatic knowledge to correlate these to the physical or emotional pathology. It's gone on for years now and, you know, there are significant relationships between the field and the illness.

OW: This is most exciting!

Dr. Laidlaw: Have you written on this, doctor?

Dr. Pierrakos: I have written, but I haven't published. It's very hard . . . for one thing this meeting for me is like nectar because I often feel isolated. If you speak out like this . . . I need very much the encouragement of colleagues.

OW: All your friends here understand what you're talking about. It's wonderful to have that gift—and in your field of healing it's invaluable.

Dr. Pierrakos: It has impressed me very deeply . . . the nature of changes in the field in relation to the illness. In very many psychosomatic disturbances the physical disturbances of the body are related to the type of aura, the pulsatory rate of the field, the color and movement.

OW: Each one is an individual.

Dr. Pierrakos: There are differences in each person but I perceive more the general characteristics. Sometimes things are very clear and the colors are very bright; other times they are not. Sometimes there are brilliant colors and they bring out the flaw. Because they bring out the flaw, the field is more visible, but when the flaw is suppressed I can't see it.

Dr. Laidlaw: When you are conducting a psychotherapeutic interview, is your visualization of the aura something which is carried on concomitantly with your psychiatric work? I mean, if you are prodding a painful area will you notice a change, which will be a signal which we psychiatrists, without such a gift, are not able to perceive?

Dr. Pierrakos: It is not always easy. Sometimes, however, it is very obvious. For instance, one thing that is very obvious to me when I look at the patient's field: the color of the first layer of the aura around the body is light blue, but when that around his head is of a dirty yellow brownish hue, I have from experience the feeling that the patient is cooking up something. He is lying or there is some kind of disturbance between the feeling and thoughts—so during most of the session we discuss these thoughts.

Schizophrenic patients have very many basic interruptions that are there all the time. There are blocks around practically every joint that prevent the flow of movement in the field and there are obstructions in the back at the neck and shoulders. . . .

Continuing to probe the more technical aspects, Ambrose spoke of a physician, a Dr. George Starr White, who had written a book entitled *The Story of the Human Aura*.[2] White, he revealed, believed that health and disease both make themselves evident in the aura, that the color of the average aura is grayish blue, and that the rays change in appearance when an individual is turned toward different points of the compass.

Dr. White's conclusions as reported by the Worralls: that aura is a matter of magnetism, apparently meaning a predominantly physical magnetism. On this, Dr. White goes into remarkable detail, claiming that his own investigations disclosed that magnetic emanations from the fourth finger of the left hand and the thumb of the right hand are positive and that the emanations from the fourth finger of the right hand and the thumb of the left hand are negative.

The role of magnetism, of the sort comparable to that of the magnetic poles, for example, is still to be explored in relationship to the psychic forces playing upon man and perhaps affecting the character—even possibly the aura of the soul—of human beings.

Ambrose also reported that Dr. White had worked with what he called an "auric cabinet" to study this phenomena.

AW (question to John Laurance[3]): Did you pick this up [about the auric cabinet], John, in any of your studies?

2. Out of print.

3. Electronics engineer; vice-president, Technation Corporation.

Mr. Laurance: Yes, it was mentioned in some of the books . . .

AW: I've got to find out what kind of a cabinet that is. John, I know you talked about a cabinet, some big cabinet to put the whole body in.

Mr. Laurance: That's just a black, dark cabinet.

AW: I don't know what kind White had. I haven't personally seen White's book.

Dr. Pierrakos: I have a copy. . . . It's a very rare book. He was a physician and I think he studied with Dr. [Albert] Abrams.[4]

OW: Will you find out just how he made that little box?

Dr. Pierrakos: I didn't see that in the book. I wish I had seen it because I'm very interested myself.

AW: Well, if it's a very rare book perhaps I'll never see it. According to Kilner,[5] the color of health is bluish gray, interchanged with yellow and red, the gray of a duller color is typical of a diseased body. Kilner preferred to base his diagnosis on the shape of the aura rather than on its chromatic qualities. Bulges in the aura indicated certain things to him. Kilner's work has been taken up and developed by Oscar Bagnall. Do you know the Bagnall work, John?

Mr. Laurance: There's a book by him.[6]

AW: Yes. He agrees that no aura shines from any dead thing. And that the outer aura is subject to radical changes brought about by mood or disease. According to Bagnall, auric light is ultraviolet; it has definite wave lengths that lie beyond the visible spectrum in the region extending from 400 millimicrons to about 310 millimicrons. The use of a blue filter tends to eliminate the longer red and orange rays of light and to emphasize the violet. Sensitizing the eye can also be achieved by first gazing at areas of yellow paper which fatigue retinal nerves to red

4. Doctor of medicine; author of *New Concepts in Diagnosis and Treatment* (San Francisco: Physico-Clinical Co., 1924); pioneer in field of radiesthesia.

5. Walter J. Kilner, *The Human Aura* (New Hyde Park, N.Y.: University Books, Inc., 1965).

6. *The Origin and Properties of the Human Aura* (London: Kegan Paul, 1937).

and green and at the same time bring out a stronger response to violet and blue.

Organic diseases seem to affect the inner aura. The emanating rays may lose their sparkle and appear dull or limpid. Intellectual or nervous disorders seem to affect the outer aura. Someday the practice of medicine and surgery may take into account the changes in the condition of health indicated by the auric emanations and give us a lot more knowledge of what's going on in disease and during the actual surgical operations under anaesthetic. . . .

Dr. Laidlaw: I talked with Phoebe Payne Bendit[7] who has worked extensively in the field. She says that she has watched a number of patients being given electric shock and the instant that the current passes (a tenth of a second) through the brain, the individual's aura is just smashed to smithereens, just like taking a kaleidoscope and shaking it, and then it gradually coalesces and reforms, and she says that this might be in some way an explanation of the therapeutic effects of electric shock.

OW: It rearranges the aura.

Dr. Laidlaw: You speak of the necessity of the healing ray penetrating the aura in order to get to the physical body. If that is really the only explanation we have, might it not work on the aura itself? You remember in Karagulla's recent book, *Breakthrough to Creativity*,[8] she describes sensitives reporting to her their observations of the human fields of energies where, in addition to energies coming out from the body, there are energies going in. Might not the healing ray affect those energies and in turn bring about a healing?

AW: Whether spiritual healing is accomplished by rays nobody knows. But is it not reasonable to suppose that some healers, having the ability to generate rays of one frequency, may be able to treat only certain types of diseases, while other healers, generating rays of a different frequency, may be effective in the treatment of other types of disorders?

7. A well-known English clairvoyant who, with her husband, Dr. Laurence J. Bendit, published a number of books in the field of parapsychology, including *The Psychic Sense* (London: Faber & Faber, 1958).

8. Shafica Karagulla, M.D., *Breakthrough to Creativity, Your Higher Sense Perception* (Los Angeles: De Vorss & Company, 1967).

We hear of healers that heal certain things and others that heal other things. Jesus Christ treated all manner of diseases very successfully. He may have had the ability to generate a number of rays of different frequencies. . . .

One conclusion emerges out of this dialogue, of significance to experts and laymen alike: The little understood role of the aura of the human being is apparently linked directly with many other fields of psychic phenomena, including that of what is now called spiritual or paranormal healing.

Some parapsychologists report that practice can develop the ability to see the emanations; that the ability is akin to learning to look in the right way, with the proper focus, to see beyond the purely physical, to see what we had not expected to see—and therefore what we could not and did not see at all.

Ambrose speaks of the "basic aura"—a force that is perhaps pristine, undefiled, totally without contact with the physical or molecular planes of reality:

The basic aura probably is in the nature of pure white light but it is colored by the personality and experiences and desires of the person, and that is why we see color in the aura. I think if you can see the aura of a newborn child, you probably would not see the reds and greens and the blues, but they would be blended into one color, which would be the color of light. How much the mother influence would be blended into that aura, I don't know. I think this would be a very interesting study also, to consider the mother's aura and the baby's aura at the same time, and as the little child becomes more and more separated from the mother, to see how the aura changes. I've never really seen the aura of a little baby and I've never seen the aura of the child and its mother at the same time.

Both Worralls agree that the average individual or student of the paranormal can learn, with the help of others perhaps more gifted, to see this emanation in its varied colorations and to interpret auric meaning. But they warn that certain major concepts should be held in mind constantly and carefully:

1. The seeming interplay of colorations and emotions signifies a direct relationship of the emotional state of the individual to psychic forces which in turn influence health, outlook, and thinking.

2. Those who could learn to see auras could also learn to understand their fellow man a little more clearly and perhaps could learn to love him even more strongly in what might be termed his "blacker moments."

3. Since the aura is apparently psychic in character, what is needed is not corrective glasses so much as the ability—and willingness—to look with the psychic inner eye.

4. The ability to see auras can be developed only slowly, with much prayer, with great discipline, with the desire not to use such areas for selfish purposes, mere amusement, or self-promotion. Here the individual is dealing with divine fire.

Because of her particularly strong love of all animals, Olga has done much psychic healing and diagnosis of dogs and cats and pet birds. In the course of the seminar discussion of auras and the life forces, the subject turned for a moment to this aspect:

> *Dr. Laidlaw*: Have you ever watched anybody in the process of death, Olga?
> *OW*: I watched . . . [interrupted by multiple conversations]
> *Dr. Laidlaw*: What happened to the aura?
> *OW*: The body lying there lifeless . . . there was no aura.
> *Q*: Have you seen animals' auras?
> *OW*: Oh yes.
> *Q*: Are they distinct?
> *OW*: Oh yes, you can feel the aura on an animal, too. Just put your hand about this much away from an animal and you can feel it.

Olga sees in her own ways, apparently, by her own unique gifts of the spirit. In animals and people—even plants—the life force is found. And in the discussion of auric force and life force, people and animals and plants intertwine in the shifting focus of questions and answers:

OW: I do want to tell of an experiment a woman made. She decided to pray over plants, so she separated the plants completely because she was told that if you have them close together some of the prayer might leak over into the next plant. So some of the plants she prayed over twice a day; she was quite sensitive and she would sense her mother's presence as she prayed. But, about the plants she was not praying over, she would say, "Oh, mother, those poor plants, I'm neglecting them. It's awful . . . I've just watered them because I feel so sorry for them." Lo and behold, the plants she felt sorry for grew twice as rapidly as those she prayed over!

James Norton:[9] Well, there's one thing that I note, since we're discussing auras, I'd suggest that . . . we've been venting our brains to try to find something, some phenomenon, that we could latch onto . . . the aura is one that we should, with proper instrumentation, be able to detect and study, and the low frequency vibration that they described is another area. I was intrigued with Ambrose's description of the aura, of the frequencies involved and the colors.

But one thing that would be fascinating—if we can capture Ambrose and Olga—is to take them into a room with some plants, a completely dark room where the rate of photosynthesis, at least the first stage reaction, and the oxygen evolution should be nil; ask them to influence the plants and if there are "effective" photons striking the plant we should have both growth and oxygen evolution in the dark. If you have oxygen evolution and carbon dioxide consumed, I think you could measure quantities of these gases pretty well, as well as the growth in the dark. . . . I think this would be interesting.

Dr. Puharich: You have a direct point there because you are saying that with respect to the actinic force, one comes from light and one comes from Ambrose, and they may be the same general type.

Mr. Norton: Yes, but what I am really interested in is the aura, and the aura is the one visible, tangible phenomenon that I think we probably could study and . . .

9. Applied physicist, General Electric Company.

Mr. Laurance: Now you're beginning to use aura in the broad sense that I like to use it—radiation plus waves.

Voice: In the aura you can see broad, visible color radiation.

Dr. Osis: Am I correct that this radiating force, in one experiment with plants, acted over a distance of one hundred yards?

AW: Yes, I'll talk about that case later. We did the praying some distance away from the laboratory in which this plant was located.

Dr. Osis: You gentlemen who are familiar with radiation—you have living matter close together and radiation—but a hundred yards is quite a distance! This is an unfamiliar force. Is it characteristic to work at such a distance?

Dr. Robert Miller:[10] Well, it's a completely different effect. One is a prayer effect and the other is an aura effect, and here we have both.

Dr. Puharich: I think that you said the recorded plant vibrations varied or something during this period.

AW: Not the plant but the needle which was indicating that something was happening to the plant.

OW: I'm going to try an experiment. Earlier we talked about auras and suddenly I had an impression to put my hands over a person. Now, let me see if you will register this . . . this is an experiment.

AW: You'd better sit down!

[Remarks and laughter]

OW: Sit a little closer. Now I'm going to do what I felt impressed to do and then you tell me . . . if you sense anything.

Voice: Seems like pressure here, possibly. You're electrostatic . . .

OW: What does that mean?

Voice: My hair was standing up.

[Laughter]

OW: No kidding!

Voice: I was kidding.

OW: Did you sense something?

Voice: Possibly a little pressure here.

OW: Now put your arms out. Sense anything?

Voice: Yes, here. I thought you were touching me.

---

10. Doctor of philosophy; research specialist in Biochemistry.

OW: No, I wasn't.

Voice: I thought it was an electrostatic . . . I couldn't differentiate it from an electrostatic effect but it felt that way. I thought you were accidentally touching me.

OW: No, no, I wasn't touching you.

Dr. Puharich: You can differentiate between that and the heat radiation?

Voice: I don't feel any sensation of heat.

Dr. Puharich: You should feel the heat at that close distance.

OW: But everybody responds differently.

Dr. Puharich: If you get within six to ten inches of me, I feel your heat immediately.

OW: Now, put *your* arms out.

Voice: Yes, I can feel you too.

OW: The very ones that will say there is nothing to it, will jump back and say, "I could feel something burning. . . ." But I was just passing through the aura.

John Laurance: You were passing through it or just on the edge of it?

OW: I was passing through it.

It is a new challenge to the psychic and the scientist alike.

Auras of the loved. Auras of the soul. Auras of the living. Reflections perhaps of what living emotions, and thought, may do or undo. Love and hate, kindness and cruelty, good and evil, the whole nature of what each of us really means and really is—echoed in the colorings of another plane of reality.

4
Laws and Superlaws

In a unique way the Worralls have examined at length the meaning of psychic fields and energies in our lives. By these energies they mean not only the metaphysical forces, but the physical as well, generated by the mind, by thought, by emotion. This involves also the laws by which such forces operate.

Ambrose does not see the two fields, psychic and physical, as dissimilar or opposed. Neither he nor Olga talks or thinks in the terminology of old-fashioned fundamentalism. Nor do they speak of the world as eternally damned.

The forces of which they speak and with which they work in healing are both physical and spiritual; they operate within both planes. The laws governing psychic forces can be experienced exactly as we explore and discover physical laws. The two are not essentially opposed.

At the start of this phase of the group discussion, Ambrose presented a new perspective of the space-time universe, a perspective understood by many of the physical-psychic school but one that is rarely if ever considered in space-program reports:

We've been passing through an age of intense concentration on the physical universe. Interest has been centered on reaching into the vast regions of space and the discovery of physical laws that govern the behavior of material substances. Science, in its careful and methodical examinations, has revealed the mechanical operations of the physical universe and as a result of these research activities, which are far from being finished, a number of present-day scientists realize that their investigations carry them across the frontier into the mysterious field of original causation.

A well-known physicist is reported to have been of the opinion that materialism had no firm foundation, that the philosophy of predetermination was a fallacy. Other scientists have also begun to speculate and suspect that some moral, ethical, and spiritual values will be found in the universe. Thus we have scientific philosophers who, through their speculations, have formed a personal religion in keeping with their scientific knowledge and inner persuasion.

In the new combined effort of science and philosophy to probe more deeply into reality, we will, in all probability, find some new theories in the field of science and some changes in religious concepts. To science we will add the personal factor and to religion we will apply the scientific method. The end result, one hopes, will be conclusive and acceptable evidence in favor of a universe of law and order, within which there is an all-pervading spiritual presence which man can intellectually acknowledge and trust. The merging of science and religion should provide a simple philosophy . . . and a knowledge of the spiritual laws, with instructions on how they must be used to benefit all.

In the light of such new knowledge we may have to discard some of the premises we have accepted in the past, abandon completely some of our practices, and develop new skills in using the immutable laws of the cosmos. Together, science and religion can give the world a God who exists in perfection, the embodiment of absolute law and order. Then man can accept logically the commandment: "Thou shalt have no other gods before me."

The art of spiritual healing involves the use of spiritual laws and applies to the improvement of conditions as well as to states of health. Much has yet to be discovered.

The fundamentals of all psychic laws, Olga declares, are present and available to us on earth; they have been given to us by the great seers across time, they have been written in the gospels of all the world's religious faiths, they have been told and retold—the "I am that I am," scrawled but still decipherable across the galaxies.

Yet still we do not know, do not accept, do not believe, do not understand.

AW: In both religion and science there are differences of opinion on how the cosmos came to be as we know it today. . . . With respect to the creation of matter, it has been said that this is brought about by use of a focusing system that, like a lens, focuses electromagnetic radiation or energy at the nodal points which mark the entry of the Cosmic Imagination into the physical world of space and time. God looking through a lens and getting it in focus, and that is how he makes creation. This is made a little clearer to the layman if we say there is a Cosmic Field which has been described as an ocean of electrical density, and which is susceptible to the influence of imagination. When the attention is properly focused on an image, the electrical field is disturbed and form waves develop, which supply the platonic archetypes which are condensed into physical form as they emerge from the Cosmic Field.

We are told that the building blocks of material universes are the elementary particles of hydrogen atoms. These particles are brought into being by the organizational capabilities of imagination and will, bringing about that trinity, space-time-energy, which is known as matter. There exists an equivalency between matter and energy as indicated in the relativity theory, but, scientifically, an explanation of the nature and origin of matter is still being sought.

Whether we refer to this ultimate environment as the Cosmic Field, the sub-ethers, the electromagnetic field, or the unified field, we are still talking about the unknown which has baffled the best scientists in their attempts to cross this frontier. We must admit that no absolute boundary, no interface between the Cosmic Field and matter, can be defined at this time; so our basic philosophy must be of a hypothetical nature.

A little later in that same statement, when the subject turns to the religio-philosophic interpretation of these laws, particularly as they relate to health and to spiritual healing, we hear another level and range of meaning:

AW: Man would be wise to give much thought to the words from the 23rd chapter of Proverbs, seventh verse, which reads: "For as he thinketh in his heart, so is he." So if a doctor tells a man a certain thing, he is going to think that way in his heart because he knows the doctor knows the truth.

Individualized man expresses his individuality by his ability to select ideas of his own choosing and show them to others in observable form through the use of his will and the law of creation. This operation of the will of man upon the idea, or that which is desired, involves faith. The principle of creative law is without limitations. The demonstration of this principle is limited by the extent of man's belief in it. The passive selection of an idea, without the act of willing it into motion, will never produce an active demonstration. Man must believe in the creative law. He must learn to trust it, to know that it always works.

This combination of belief and trust is the foundation of faith, the kind of faith that Jesus spoke of when he said: "If ye had faith as a grain of mustard seed, ye might say unto this sycamine tree, Be thou plucked up by the root, and be thou planted in the sea; and it should obey you." That's from the 17th chapter of St. Luke, sixth verse. Since man cannot escape the results of the operation of creative law, he is temporarily limited to such experiences as he has already created. By selecting new ideas and motivating them he can bring about such changes in his condition, environment, and activities that creative law will allow. . . .

Reality is in the imperceptable. Man makes the error of seeing the effect as reality whereas the Cause is reality. Looking upon effect as reality brings confusion to man's mind. The enormous complexity of effect is so great that man's mind cannot encompass it. Yet man can think of Cause, the single source of all manifestation, God, without being overwhelmed with the multiplicity of formulas applicable to effect.

But the Worralls do not merely talk—they also test and try and examine, through prayer, through spiritual treatment of patients (always in conjunction with the medical profession), and through exploration of the results and of the conditions under which they were obtained.

Both are convinced that it is only by understanding the inter-relationship of the psychic and physical fields that man can become most effective in his use of the wholeness of the gift of life.

An example of this interrelationship is seen in Dr. Robert Miller's experiment on the effect of prayer on plant growth. Dr. Miller called the Worralls from Atlanta in one instance to discuss a plant on which earlier successful psychic experiments had been demonstrated. As Ambrose reported it to the seminar:

On January 4 of this year, Thursday night at seven o'clock in the evening, Dr. Miller called us from Atlanta, Georgia, and said he had the plant stabilized again under laboratory conditions and it was growing then at a steady rate day and night of 6.25 mils per hour.[1] He said he would like to try an experiment on the plant. He asked us to set a time when we would "pray" for the plant. Accordingly, two hours later, at the time agreed upon (9:00 P.M.), Olga and I turned our attention to the plant. Turning of our attention to the person or object is our method of prayer. We continued this until 9:05 P.M. This we can look upon as five minutes of "absent" treatment.

The results of the experiment were reported to us in Dr. Miller's letter dated January 7, 1968, in which he states: "This is to let you know that the plant experiment in which you participated last week was most successful." He provided a copy of the growth rate curve on the recorder chart. This showed that the laboratory controlled rate of 6.25 mils per hour was maintained through 9:00 P.M., at which time the rate began to increase, finally reaching a rate of 52.5 mils per hour by approximately 8:00 A.M. the next morning. Thereafter, the rate of growth began to slow down. Simple arithmetic shows that the rate of growth increased to 8.4 times the laboratory controlled rate.

No one was in the building where the plant was located at the time he called, at seven o'clock at night. So in his letter he says that

1. A mil is 1/1000 of an inch.

"Now we have conclusive proof that the prayer time at nine o'clock really works and has been scientifically indicated by the increase in rate of growth of the plant."

I think this is a very startling thing. We have, of course, tried to figure out what happened, what made the growth rate increase at precisely nine o'clock. I don't think you could even do this by shooting some fertilizer into it. How could you time it so that it would suddenly increase and how could you possibly get an increase in growth of 8.4 times what it was doing previously? I think we have areas here that require a lot of investigation.

Dr. Laidlaw: Have you repeated that in any way since then?

AW: No, I haven't heard from Dr. Miller since then.

Dr. Laidlaw: I'm passing that chart around.

AW: It is so difficult to be able to settle something in the laboratory like this and prove it, you know, and I've waited fifty years to be able to do something like this. Finally, we got a scientist interested enough to put in the time and effort to make the test.

Here was an instance in which the correlation of the prayer, the blessing of God invoked, of love, of concern, for a plant was suddenly and dramatically accompanied by a change in growth rate so extraordinary that no possible "coincidence" explanation would seem to suffice.

Something apparently took effect across hundreds of miles, from Baltimore to Atlanta. Dr. Miller is a man of scientific interests and is not given to exploiting credulity or indulging in practical jokes. The measurements are made by scientific devices. Hundreds of similar experiences have, of course, also been recorded, although few if any have been more dramatic.

What then happened? How? What forces are we talking about that may work here? What kind of force field may be involved? Ambrose declared:

AW: The distance between the prayer group and the plant, measured in a straight line, is more than 600 miles. If you try to measure the effect of any force fields that emanate from a person operating at a distance of over 600 miles, you're getting involved in problems resembling some satellite experiments. It is different from radar because that is an impulse sent out and impulse reflected back, and I'm sure we all know that the power, in this case, varies inversely as the square of the distance. The power diminishes as the distance increases. In spiritual healing and in this plant experiment, we do not know how distance affects the force. It is an area of research that I hope we can enter into some day and find out just what happens.

Dr. Laidlaw: Ambrose, you say you prayed for the plant. What was your actual ideation? Was it an encouragement of growth, or what?

AW: No, we turned our attention to the plant, just like you would casually watch a TV program or look at a plant that was growing. We did not put forth any effort whatsoever, and this is back in line with my theory that if you get yourself out of the way the power will work.

OW: But you were focusing; you were putting your attention on the plant at that particular moment; the plant was in mind. Does that explain it?

Dr. Laidlaw: Yes.

AW: I think you might say that our attention probably creates a carrier wave and that this other force, whatever it is, modulates that carrier wave in some way and is carried through and does its work at the other end.

Question: Could it do the opposite? Suppose it was a weed you wanted to destroy?

AW: I think it would work that way, too. But we are very, very careful never to tune in on destructive thinking. The problem with that would be that if we started to experiment in that direction, thousands of people tuned in to us might be affected. We don't know enough about the mechanism yet. It may work on plants, and it may work on a patient who is attuned to us at that time. So we are afraid to experiment. I'm sure it would work the other way, yes. . . .

Q: Is it possible that Dr. Miller acted as a channel?

AW: Yes, he could have.

OW: You see, it was an experiment he set up and he had to know the precise time that we were projecting our thought.

Voice: Possibly his being in the proximity of the plant. . . .

AW: He was at home; he lives several miles from the building where the plant was located and was not there at the time the experiment was conducted.

Modern experimentation in plant prayer has offered a remarkable area for the study of these forces. The startling findings indicate that there are laws at work that we had best come to understand and respect. At the same time, some of the results have overtones that rival the fantastic emanations of science fiction.

At one seminar session Ambrose and Olga discussed the work of Mr. Cleve Backster of New York City, an expert in the use of polygraph instrumentation for lie detection, who conducts police officer training courses on the law-enforcement applications of the polygraph. Since 1946 Backster also has conducted experiments involving the use of the psychogalvanic reflex portion of the polygraph for measuring changes in plant life, which closely resemble reflex reactions received from humans emotionally stimulated.

The Worralls described Backster's initial observation when he had intention of burning a plant leaf being tested. The plant tracing, precisely timed with the mere thought of burning of the leaf, leaped into intense activity, nearly traveling off the moving chart paper. This observation was repeated, each time involving a different plant. Where actual harm was not inflicted on a plant, a second attempt on the same plant would not produce a similar type reaction. It seemed apparent that the plant could differentiate between sincere intent to inflict harm and pretense of such intent.

Here, it would appear, we are touching on laws that appertain to levels of reality most of us have not yet reached. We catch flashes of these laws, perhaps intuitions, we have episodes in which they seem to be involved.

Sometimes, almost unwittingly, Ambrose will speak of these laws. He will talk of "tuning in" on someone else's wave length in order to help heal that person; he will speak also of crossing into another dimension of time or space. He has described episodes in which others—reputable, reliable citizens—reported to him that he had been in their home or room the night before—when he knew that he had not physically been there.

We tend to think of the laws and superlaws of the universe as remote and beyond the use or need of average individuals. The fact is that we are talking about laws that exist for all of us—laws that serve humanity, laws we must learn to understand.

Olga, herself, is essentially a very normal individual, housewife and good neighbor, who loves to tend her plants and grows some of the loveliest flowers on the block in the Baltimore suburb where she and Ambrose live.

Olga also makes use of her understanding of the laws—frequently in a down-to-earth way that is often amusing, startling, and wholly refreshing:

Dr. Laidlaw: Olga, what is this about your preparing plants for a flower show?

OW: Oh boy, I'm sneaky!

Voice: Now I know how to win a blue ribbon!

AW: She's won many ribbons.

OW: Yes, I was horticulture chairman of our garden club and we used all my own plants in making arrangements. But I talk to my plants; you may think it's foolish but I do talk to them; I actually feel something coming from my plants. On this particular occasion we were having a special class in coxcombs, the feathery and the broad. The Garden Club was depending on my garden and it had been a very wet spring. The seeds weren't doing very well and what few plants came up were straggly and sad-looking things, so I took two of these seedlings out and put them in a separate part of the garden and I said to them, "Now, I want you to grow beautifully for me because if you do you'll be entered in the flower show." Every morning when I'd go out to the garden with Ambrose I'd talk to them and thank them and tell them they were making good progress, then during the day I'd go out and look at them. Their growth was phenomenal compared to the other plants.

The day before the flower show I was given the measurements that were needed, you know, so many inches tall, in order to compete with other entries. I was lacking an inch for the coxcomb, the broad coxcomb. So I thought, "Oh my golly, what am I going to do?" I went out to the coxcomb and I said, "Look, I need an inch more; come on, how about it. Grow real good overnight and tomorrow you'll go to the flower show *if* you have enough length." Well, when I went out to cut the coxcomb I had more length than was needed. I entered the coxcombs in the flower show and received first prize ribbons for both of them. They were beautiful . . . the yellow feathery . . . it was magnificent. There were three garden clubs that participated. Of all the coxcombs displayed mine were the most beautiful.

One session on these force fields and laws Ambrose and Olga gave largely to psychometry—the emanations that tell the "sensitive" something of this object, who owned it, what it signified if anything at all.

With usual thoroughness, Ambrose in this statement probed deeply into the ramifications of this kind of energy and its sources:

Let us turn our attention to inanimate objects. We know of course that force fields exist around commonly known things like a magnet, a copper wire carrying electric current, and uranium. Sensitive persons are also aware of emanations from articles which can be of almost any kind of materials, in the natural state or fabricated by man. The term given to the faculty that is capable of detecting and analyzing these emanations is psychometry; and one who possesses and uses this faculty is commonly referred to as a psychometrist.

Spiritual healing has throughout history been accomplished in conjunction with blessed articles, such as prayer cloths, crosses, stones, holy books, relics, water, shrines, statues, paintings, and other things. Strange though it may seem, articles can also be associated with misfortune rather than blessings.

There is an interesting example of the apparent effect of the force field of an inanimate article in the Greek legend of Cadmus and Harmonia. At their wedding, the wife, Harmonia, was given a necklace which had the property of stirring up strife and bloodshed, thus bringing evil to every possessor. It was said that the necklace was made by Hephaestus, God of Fire, whose cult was introduced into Athens about six hundred years before Christ.

We can say that this story is only a legend, but references can be made to another famous article of modern times, the Hope Diamond, associated with the misfortune of all who possessed it.

In this electronic age we are accustomed to the use of the term "memory banks," in connection with data-processing equipment. It is possible that similar banks exist in all inanimate articles, that these banks store the bits of data flashed to them throughout the history of the article, and that under certain conditions these memory banks can be tapped and the data read by a psychometrist.

If a material object or article of clothing is used by a living person, it comes under the influence of that person's force field. There is reason to believe that his health, thoughts, acts, skills, experiences, and the high points of his life are recorded in the memory banks of the material.

When such an article is passed from its original owner to another living person, that person may respond in some manner to its influence. The extent of his response and the nature of its effect upon him depends upon his ability to read data in its memory banks.

Every living person has developed, over his period of existence, a sensitivity to certain stimuli of a mental nature. The nature of the stimuli to which he responds depends upon his experiences and the types of thoughts that he entertains.

In this theoretical conception we assume that the article has memory banks with infinite capacity. They receive data in sequential time and store it in whole time. When the article is brought into coupling range with a sensitive who is *en rapport* with it, the knowledge stored in whole time is revealed to the psychometrist in a flash. Associated with this type of psychometry is foretelling of future events, the reason being that future events are already in existence in whole time and are revealed along with historical events that occur in sequential time.

It is not only the gift of psychic powers that is essential for results; it is also the individual's life experience, his concern, his outlook.

He develops in large measure as he gives himself to dedicated purpose and service.

He thus becomes, in some limited measure, a channel of help, of guidance, of communication.

The nature of the laws by which individuals with special gifts can effect changes in physical conditions and physical objects is one of the key question marks in the examination of the psychic-physical syndrome.

If what the Worralls say and do is valid—and here it is often difficult even to raise an effective challenge—then one is forced to accept the reality of some form of interrelationship of the normal and paranormal in our lives.

Part of the seminar discussions on laws and force fields of energy concerned some experiments with distilled water in which Ambrose had placed his hands around a container of water, in effect giving power and affirmation through his hands and through the container into the water itself.

At one point in the discussion of this treated water, a segment of the colloquy ran:

AW: The question about Dr. Miller raises the thought about the person who is acting as an intercessor for a sick person, who may be in a coma, or too sick, or too young to understand. Yes, I do think these people do act as relay stations through which the power flows.

Dr. Puharich: Ambrose, on the contrary, you have Dr. Grad's[2] experiments where they had double blinds and the person who was pouring the water, the treated and untreated water, didn't really know which water was treated or untreated, and there only the treated water had an effect. In effect you moved the intercessor, the organism, and put it into the water, so, in a way, that question has been looked at by Dr. Grad.

AW: There's another thing that Dr. Miller told me when I was down at Atlanta the last time. We had to change planes at Atlanta. We'd

2. Dr. Bernard Grad has been carrying on research at McGill University, Montreal, on the effect of laying-on-of-hands on plant growth.

been down at West Palm Beach lecturing and on the way back we changed planes and, during the stopover, we saw him for fifteen minutes. He told us the story about the water that I had treated, which we discussed the last time he was here, and he found out that the treated water stored in the polyethylene bottle and the treated water stored in the glass bottle had different resistances. Now, you see, I would never have thought about them being stored in different containers.

Q: Did he get a different effect?

AW: Yes, he told me that the resistances were different and they were the same batch of treated distilled water. I don't know just where this experiment is leading him now, but he did tell this to me when I was there, at the Atlanta airport.

Q: Just to get it clear, the water in the polyethylene bottle was not treated?

AW: The water was in a glass flask when it was treated; a portion was then poured into a polyethylene bottle. Incidentally, the first flask he brought, when I put my hands around it, I said, "This is radioactive." He said, "There's nothing in there but distilled water." And I said, "Well, I can't help it, it's radioactive." And it didn't show any reading on the Geiger counter when he checked it. However, when he checked the history of the flask he found that it had contained carbon 14, which is mildly radioactive, and evidently the flask itself had picked up some of this radioactivity and I registered it with my hands, which is an indication of the supersensitivity of the human being. So he got another flask, a smaller one, containing some of the same water, and I treated that. He did tell me that he had poured some of this water onto the plant just that day, when we talked with him while we were changing planes. But he hadn't had time to see whether any effect had been registered on the growth of the plant.

I asked him whether he had made any other tests on the water, and he said he had poured some of the water into a pie plate, that he had gotten some special photographic film from a photographer and put it over the pie plate and left it there all through the weekend. The photographer told him he couldn't possibly get any reaction on this film from distilled water in a pie plate. What he actually got was a photograph of the pie plate and water, which they have been unable to explain. This was special photographic film which was sensitive only in the high ultraviolet range, so I suppose they're still trying to figure out what happened. I asked him, "Did you take some untreated water and try the same thing with film?" But he hadn't done that. He said he would try the same experiment with untreated water. So we're on the way to some experiments anyway, and maybe from the results we might learn something of the nature of the forces at work.

Much work is being done in this field of psychic energy, protective energy, healing energy, communication, astral elements that transport themselves seemingly across time and space barriers—the whole pattern of force, movement, space-time relationships, at both tangible and intangible levels.

The answer to the riddle is not easy to piece together.

Sometimes, even in these difficult areas of investigation, a single meaningful episode can say more than a thousand or so scientific words.

This incident, as related by Ambrose to the seminar session, concerned a visit a medical physician[3] and a scientist investigator from Philadelphia made to Baltimore to attempt some tests with the Worralls:

AW: . . . They developed a number of experiments with magnets and went through a series of tests with a sensitive in California. Then they came to Baltimore and put us through the same tests, and the results were similar to the ones they got in California. We were able to detect, for instance, which way the magnetic field was flowing at the end of a bar magnet.

There was another experiment that I think might be of very great interest. Dr. F had one of the Melpar[4] scientists construct a broadcasting unit, what you might call a little black box—in this case it wasn't black, but what we used to call black boxes in electronic language. There were a number of knobs and switches on the black box and by

---

3. The physician authorized the use of the story but requested that his name not be used. We refer to him hereafter simply as Dr. F.

4. A large Delaware electronics firm.

adjusting these things he could broadcast, on the short aerial, different frequencies. The power that came from this aerial was so small that it could barely be detected on the finest instruments available for detecting radio waves. Dr. F squatted on the floor with his little black box and he draped the aerial over the couch. Olga sat on the couch near the aerial and I sat in a chair on the other side of the aerial. Dr. F had determined that at certain frequencies there should be effects in specific parts of the human body. He switched on the current and he turned the knobs and we certainly felt effects, in the throat, the top of the head, down in the feet, in the thighs and different places. Now this went on for quite a long time, and when he got through he said, "Well, I tried everything to catch you people. I was not able to catch you because every time I set it in a certain place I got the same answer." And here again you have this very small amount of force which is picked up by the human body.

OW: How about that experiment in the basement, with sound waves or something?

AW: When he brought the mice over?

OW: Those mice!

AW: Dr. F is very interested in cancer research. He tries everything nobody else has tried. He decided to try the effect of magnetic fields upon cancer-prone mice. He had the same Melpar scientist make a magnetic coil, through the heart of which he had a polyethylene tube about three inches in diameter. He had this coil hooked up with what is called a breadboard version of electronic circuitry, which consisted of a number of different modules which could be interconnected in different ways by means of alligator clips so they would provide different frequencies. They hooked the circuits up to an oscilloscope, their purpose being to have Olga state which were the best frequencies to use in treating these cancer-prone mice because, they said, they could go on for fifty years on all the different frequencies before hitting on the right one.

Olga was sitting there and they said, "How is that frequency?" and she said, "That's no good. It has to be much higher than that." So they kept changing these clips around and moving the rate up to higher and higher frequencies until she said, "Now that is the right frequency." She then gave the number of cycles. This Melpar man looked up and said, "How do you know?" He read the oscilloscope, checked all of his connections, and he referred to his book and found that the frequency was indeed the number of cycles stated by Olga.

So how did she pick it up? I don't know. Maybe somewhere out there in the unseen, there was an intelligence that knew what the frequency was and transmitted this information to Olga.

5
Body and Soul

What metaphysicians speak of as the astral body is not to be confused with auric emanations. The living human body and the astral body both have auras, according to statements of the Worralls and others at the Wainwright sessions. But the astral body is not itself merely an emanating energy dependent on something else; it is a source of energy, rather; it is an identity; it is the substance of the soul.

The metaphysical debate centering around this issue is considered of extreme importance. In essence the question becomes: Is there such a thing as the astral body? Are we talking of ghosts, phantoms, spirits that wander around while their bodies sleep? Is there either voluntary or involuntary extracorporeal travel? Or is it all merely superstition, remnants of folklore, fear, and ignorance?

What makes the problem both more interesting and more difficult is the residue of superstition, self-deception, and unverifiable claims on the one side—and a wide revival of concern and serious investigation on the other. Discoveries regarding the role of ESP, scientific investigations in psychic phenomena by governments, colleges, universities, and independent workers, the wealth of information accumulating in parapsychological researches, particularly those conducted in association with physicians and practicing psychiatrists—all of this has opened the door to entirely new approaches to the true nature of this so-called astral being.

From an outside, objective point of view, no definitive determination has been reached. Among persons deeply concerned in this field, such as those at the seminars, there are wide-ranging views and counterviews. Yet the majority appear to accept as basic the postulate that the soul of the individual human being not only exists but exists—and persists—in some degree as an individual, as some form of entity.

To Ambrose Worrall, more perhaps than to any other living sensitive of our time, reality of the astral body is clear and beyond challenge. In Ambrose's own words one catches a totality of awareness, understanding, and communication. Yet the certainty of his words is edged by the difficulty of articulating these ideas, out of another plane, to human understanding and limitation:

AW: The astral body, or spiritual body, is the seat of sensation. All sensation is in the astral, not the physical, body. When you hypnotize a person, you are extracting the spiritual body from the physical body. That's why you can hypnotize a person, for instance, and take away pain from his arm merely by verbal command. There's a separation there of the spiritual from the physical, but the arm does not die because there is always what they call the silver cord, which binds the spiritual to the physical. Until that cord is severed, the life forces will still be maintained in the physical body. That's why some people can be in a coma for twenty years; the body is still theirs as long as it is nourished and taken care of because the silver cord has not been severed.

The astral body is the same size as the physical body, and we all leave the physical body when we go to sleep. It's just another way of separation; you can do it by sleep; you can do it by drugs; you can do it by shock; you can do it by hypnosis. The astral body, so long as it's connected with the cord, can receive information about what is going on in the physical body, and although it cannot feel pain, it still knows what is going on. It is as though the silver cord conveys information not feeling. But when the spiritual body is coincided properly with the physical body, then it is aware of all the conditions of the physical body. I believe it is true that if an organ is healthy you are not aware of its existence, but you immediately become aware of a part of your body when there's something wrong with it. In a pure, healthy, natural state you are not aware of any part of your body; and when you're out in the spiritual body, you are not aware of any aches and pains or any of those things which you feel when you are back in the body.

Now the physical body responds to the spiritual body—after all that's the matrix on which it was built—and I think the spiritual body is greatly affected by the way a person thinks; I think the orbits of all the electrons, protons, neutrons, and whatever you have in there . . . all respond to the condition of the spiritual body, which in itself is affected by the way people think and their emotions. This is the source of illness, and we can destroy ourselves by our way of thinking or we can limit ourselves. So I think we can get down to where you can say that practically everything is probably psychosomatic.

Why does a person have an accident? Perhaps because he had fear, or some destructive thought came into his consciousness for some reason, causing him, for example, to step out into the street where he is hit by an automobile, whereas if he hadn't had that condition of mind, something would have prevented him from stepping out into the street at that time.

The spiritual body is the vehicle through which you function when you go to sleep. Going to sleep is the same as dying except the silver cord is not severed. Dying is just as easy and simple as going to sleep, so you should have no fear of it. However, the state of mind has much to do with death, and if you could die without any qualms— then you are likely to live to be one hundred and fifty. It's as simple as that.

Now at the time of death, the proper thing that should happen is that you just step out of this overcoat of the physical body because you are going where you won't need it any longer. If you have no further use for it, you graduate into this other dimension for which you should have prepared yourself in the development of your spiritual faculties, and go on with the feeling, "Well, I did the best I could when I was on earth. I tried not to think too much about myself. . . . I did try to fill that niche in the scheme of things for which I felt I was fitted. I tried to feel that I was a part of all humanity. . . . Even though I recognized my individuality, I tried to feel that I was part of the whole and that I benefited the whole by my existence. Therefore, I made a contribution to the benefit of all mankind."

If we can go over with this kind of thought, we are ready to continue the progression which is possible in the other life. . . . But if we don't do this, if we pass away with some reservations in our mind, then this acts like a weight that drags us down and keeps us down to the lower levels, where we try to repay, or to carry out, the things we should have done in this life on earth.

These are among the things that should be taught in churches. To try to control people by fear is wrong. We must point out to them the lasting benefits of following a constructive path and living the progressive life on earth because this is only one phase of the life that continues after death. I think this is important and it would appeal to the intelligence of the younger people today, who are scientifically oriented and very interested in ESP.

OW: For instance, Dr. Laidlaw is handicapped because of the polio that he suffered but his astral body is perfect, and when you go to sleep at night and you dream and walk about, you're not handicapped. Correct? And your astral body is perfect.

When there is a disease of some sort, if you can effect perfect alignment and meshing of the astral body with the physical body it assists in the healing process.

Dr. Laidlaw: If you do that the result is what?

OW: In cases of illness, the astral body being perfect tries to manifest that perfection in the physical body.

One questioner raised the issue of when and how control of the astral body can be developed or obtained by the physical entity:

Voice: In other words, some individuals can have astral projection: some during sleep, some that is chemically induced, and others produced by death. What about voluntary control of this body?

AW: Of the natural or astral body?

Voice: Is there a dividing line—a certain phase at which the physical individual is unable to control the presence or absence of the astral body and at another time quite able to project himself?

AW: Everything works according to law. Under hypnosis, under drugs, you cannot keep the astral body in the physical body. Drugs, chloroform, ether, drive the astral body out of the physical body so it cannot be controlled under those conditions. It obeys what I call the perfect law.

Now, as far as astral travel is concerned—some people call it mind travel but there's a difference between mind travel and astral travel. You can only explain it if you have the experience. Everybody travels when they go to sleep except those that are so tied down by interests on the earth that it holds them to the earth and they do not travel away from their interests. The miser, after he goes to sleep, will hover around his gold.

We travel to those regions for which we have fitted ourselves by our type of thinking, our desires. We travel to that level in the spiritual environment for which we are fitted by our spiritual specific gravity. If we are loaded down with the things of the earth, we will stay close to the earth. If we are more interested in the things of the spirit, we will rise high in the spiritual realm. The problem is that if you rise too high in the spiritual realm, it is so beautiful that you don't want to come back. However, you have a duty to perform here and you should live out your natural span. To the extent that we can control our spiritual specific gravity, to that extent we can control where our spiritual body goes.

Regarding astral travel, if you want to will yourself to go to a certain place you will probably go there, but to bring the memory of that journey back across the threshold of the physical or waking consciousness is not easy. As the astral or spiritual body comes close to the physical body, you experience a whirling sensation as you are re-coinciding with the physical, and during that whirling sensation you forget where you have been in the astral travel.

It may be quite fortunate in some cases that we are not allowed to remember. But, having traveled in my spiritual body and been permitted to remember, I know that it is possible. I have not only traveled and remembered but I have been seen by other people in these places where I have traveled, and I've even had people feel my hands upon them giving them treatments. Now I have never really tried to control my astral travel by saying, "I will go to a specific place. I will record what is going on there." I don't seem to have any real control over this, but I have had sufficient experience to know that it can be done.

Ambrose admits that his knowledge in this activity is shadowed by the fact that his experience has been in a large degree involuntary. He described his own first (and somewhat embarrassing) episode of this sort:

AW: My first knowledge of astral travel was when my father called me into the store back in England—I was maybe sixteen or seventeen—there was a lady in the store and she accused me of being in her bedroom at night. I thought she was completely out of her mind; I didn't even know the woman and I didn't know where she lived. She said, "You stay out of my bedroom at night." I said, "I've never been in your bedroom, lady. I don't know where you live. I don't even know who you are." She said, "Every night when I put out the light you are standing at the foot of my bed." I thought she was deranged, but later when I had experiences of astral travel and remembered them, my mind went back to this lady and I thought that maybe what she said was true. I *was* wandering around, but what was I doing there in *that* lady's bedroom and what was the purpose of my visits? These things were never revealed to me. Astral travel is something that some people say they can do at will. I have not been able to do it at will.

Q: Do you feel any particular sensations during the period when you're assisting people and helping cure them?

AW: Yes, when I have my hands on the person, whatever is coming out of my hands feels like thick warm air. People say that my hands feel like hot pads. A lady explained it as feeling like the second heat on a heating pad. I don't know where this heat comes from. It's not because I've been rubbing my hands or massaging people. I just put my hands on them and suddenly this heat starts to build up and it seems to be coming out of my hands. When I'm in a spiritual healing condition—although I know my hand is on the person—it feels to me that it is slightly away from the person's body. I reason from this that my spiritual body is slightly dissociated from the physical body when I am in the healing situation. I actually have two reasons for saying this: One is that when I have my hands on the person, my hands do not have the normal sensation of contact. The second one is that my body has no sense of weight whatsoever, and no sense of tiredness. I know

my body is there but it's like a shadow . . . it doesn't mean anything. . . . Perhaps this slight dissociation is necessary in order for
the power to flow freely. I have felt also a tingling sensation like a thousand electric sparks coming out of my hands.

Voice: Like the shock when you touch an electric wire?

AW: No! Like a lot of needle points pricking my hands. I had
this experience with a Lebanese scientist. His technician was a young
lady who had picked up a fungus condition under the nail of the index
finger. When the nail grew out it always grew out with the affected
part eaten away. They were working in Johns Hopkins Hospital, where
scrapings were taken and examined. They knew what the fungus was.
They said, as far as they were concerned, it was incurable. They tried
everything they knew, X-ray treatments and different kinds of medication, but without success.

The Lebanese scientist invited his technician and us to his home
to view some slides on Lebanon. Before the showing of the slides he
referred to the technician's fungus problem and said: "Here we have
what we call a controlled experiment. We know exactly what this
young lady's problem is with the fingernail. We have tried everything
known in medicine and we've been unable to cure it. Do you think
you can do anything with it?"

I said, "I don't know, go ahead and show your slides." While he
was showing the slides, I held the diseased finger in my hand and
listened to him tell about the slides he had taken in Lebanon. I felt
as though a thousand needles were pricking the palm of my hand, but
I wasn't paying much attention to it as I was interested in Lebanon,
where I've never been. After the slides were over I released the girl's
finger and put on the lights. The inflammation was gone. When the
nail grew out it was perfect.

There you had a controlled experiment in which a cure was
effected. It was a very simple thing, but how it was done, we don't
know. If you knew how it was done, then you could repeat it. Maybe
if we could find out what it is that flows from a healer's hands we could
duplicate it in some manner. The X-ray tube is nothing but a mechanical
clairvoyant—an electric clairvoyant, right? Maybe they can make some
kind of a gadget—maybe it will come out of electronics—which would
duplicate what flows out of the healer's hands. . . .

Voice: At one point there it seemed to me that you were saying, or might be saying, that your etheric body was in contact with the patient's etheric body and that you had completely forgotten the somatic body.

AW: Yes, I believe that during healing administrations the contact is between the astral bodies of healer and patient. Consciousness of the somatic body is attenuated during this time.

Both Olga and Ambrose, it must be kept in mind, are sensitives, each in a specific way. They are both healers. Both have a variety of psychic gifts. What they experience and what they achieve seemingly cannot be duplicated by everyone else—just as not all of us can learn to play the piano at the level of a great pianist.

The interrelationship of these two sensitives, as revealed in the discussions at Wainwright, is in itself unique.

But what they share also is the life of the spirit, the life of another plane where experience is wholly different, the psychic plane of healing:

Q: Mr. Worrall, do you think that the mechanism that operates when a person is healed from the distance is similar to that with the plants—praying for the plants?

AW: Yes, I think it's the same type of operation. The mechanism is the same but I don't know what it is. It violates all the physical laws we know about operating forces at a distance.

Dr. Puharich: Do you think the action is directly in the astral body and only secondarily in the physical, or do you think there is an action on the physical itself? I mean that which we commonly call the physical body.

AW: I don't really know.

Dr. Puharich: Suppose you watch Olga healing somebody or vice versa and you are looking at the astral body or the aura or something, are you able to detect any action that occurs that results in objective healing?

AW: I usually see it as a manifestation in the physical when I detect a change. I see the color come back to the face and the eyes getting brighter. These are the kind of things I see. But I don't know whether it works directly on the physical body or on the astral body or on both.

OW: Very often . . . if I'm in that clairvoyant state—one is not always clairvoyant—but sometimes in a clairvoyant state I find that the astral body of the person is not in full coordination with the physical body and there is trouble. You will find that there is quite a dislodgment in the area where there is trouble. And I mentally say, "Come on, get back into your body." I find that when it finally takes full possession of the physical body, the healing manifests in the physical body. . . .

As a rule Ambrose does his healing without my presence. I'm downstairs and he's with the patient in the healing room. But I really feel that the astral is a very important vehicle for carrying that healing. . . .

AW: You see, there are so many systems generated. The onion has a lot of skins. We talk about the physical body and etheric body and the mental body. Perhaps you have to divide the thing up in this way in order to make a system like theosophy. Perhaps there are people who have observed all these different levels. It's like the mind. We divide the mind up into the subconscious, the subliminal mind, the conscious mind, and the superconscious. It is still the mind, but in order to examine it you divided it up into these different areas. Now the only things that we know about in our experience are the physical body and the spiritual body, also called the astral body.

I have seen two things: (1) the body of a person who no longer lives in his physical body, and (2) the body of a person who still lives in the physical body, and when I say body, I'm talking about the spiritual body. I have traveled astrally, as we call it, in my spiritual body. I have been seen in my spiritual body by people on earth.

OW: I, myself, have seen Ambrose's astral body at a time when he has been out of town on business, standing by the bedside awakening me, hearing his voice. I would see him and speak with him and then he would disappear. On one occasion he awakened me. I saw him standing by the bed. He projected the thought: "Put out the light in the bathroom." I kept getting that pounded into my mind. Finally I got out of bed and switched off the light in the bathroom. This was the only time in all our married life that I had a light burning in the house after retiring when Ambrose was not home. Ambrose told me later that he found himself in our living room. He said it was so real that he didn't realize he was in his astral body.

Q: You remembered it afterward?

AW: Yes, I remembered it.

OW: Oh, yes, because as soon as he came in the house after his return from the trip, he said, "I had a very strange experience." I immediately said, "Yes, I know, you came home and made me put the light out in the bathroom."

Dr. Puharich: Were you asleep at the time?

AW: Yes, I was asleep. I was in Dayton, Ohio.

Dr. Puharich: When you referred earlier, Ambrose, to the experience of being seen elsewhere, although you yourself were not aware of it, I'm sure you can associate this with a similar type of phenomenon, which is known as the *vardøgr* in Norway, and probably in the Hebrides and some parts of Scotland. The general pattern of the phenomenon is that, let's say, a man has a regular time to go from his office to his home, and it seems quite common in many families for the father to be seen coming as his shadow self or double, when he is physically not there. This has been seen individually and collectively by people outside the family. Is this the sort of thing you were referring to when you were seen elsewhere but you, yourself, were unaware of being there?

AW: Yes . . . it appears to be similar in some cases but not all. For instance, the first experience called to my attention, when I was around the age of sixteen or seventeen, involved appearance in a place with which I was unfamiliar.

OW: We have had people write and say they were experiencing great pain and called Ambrose mentally, after which they felt Ambrose's hands on their back or on their head. Or they saw Ambrose right in the room standing beside their bed, fell asleep, and upon awakening all the pain had disappeared. We've had a number of letters from people who have seen Ambrose in his spiritual body. I may also be doing that but I do not recall the experience. Several women have told me that they were awakened in the middle of the night and felt me placing my hands on their head.

AW: When I awake in the morning I know occasionally that I have been doing work on the spiritual level, involving out-of-the-body experiences.

In the theory of astral flight or projection, as described by many metaphysicians and writings in this field, the concept of the silver or umbilical cord that ties the astral to the physical body has wide acceptance. The cord is considered to be a link from one plane to another, the physical and the spiritual. Students of this theory of a psychic silver cord warn of peril that exists in astral travel should this cord be severed during the journey. Such a separation, it is asserted, would be fatal to the physical body. Olga relates the story of a child in India who was believed to be dead and was brought back to life by the ministrations of an Indian holy man. The question was raised at the seminar: Was this child in fact dead or was it a case of suspended animation? The discussion of the group turned then to the basic nature of the cord, this psychic, possibly ectoplasmic, link between body and soul:

OW: The child was not actually "dead." This holy man could see that the silver cord had not been severed, so it was possible to restore life to the physical body.

Voice: Then the child wasn't dead.

OW: Apparently she wasn't dead. The holy man said, "She will come back." Yet according to the medical report, the child was dead. But the cord hadn't been severed, so the holy man was able to bring the spirit back into the body.

Voice: Perhaps many people are buried who are not really dead when the doctors say they are.

OW: There have been cases reported where persons declared dead have been found to be alive. We should be absolutely sure the cord is severed before writing the death certificate.

Q: In your experience, is there any way any of us could tell whether a person really is dead or not? . . .

OW: Well, I haven't had much experience with bodies at the time of clinical death and what takes place immediately thereafter, but I have observed a few people that were ready to pass away where the spirit was out of the physical body and the silver cord was so thin it was ready to snap.

Dr. Laidlaw: The cord between the physical and astral bodies?

OW: Yes, connecting the astral body with the physical body.

Dr. Laidlaw: And the astral body was at a distance?

OW: Yes, you can see that must be so or the astral body and the physical body would still be blended together, and the cord would not be visible.

Q: Where is the cord? At what point . . . ?

OW: It's like an umbilical cord, like that which joins a newly born baby to its mother. The astral cord is attached centrally right in the solar plexus. I've had several experiences where I have seen the cord just elongate and thin out.

Q: Once the cord does separate, what happens to the astral body?

OW: It will fade away from the earthbound observer, the clairvoyant, as the cord disintegrates. . . .

Dr. Julius Chepko:[1] But I thought the astral body was something different from the spirit. I thought the spirit occupied the astral body and, in turn, the astral body resides in the physical.

OW: That's right.

Dr. Chepko: Then the astral body disintegrates in time?

OW: No, it's the vehicle that the spirit functions through. The real you functions through the astral body.

Dr. Chepko: Yes, but in time the astral body disintegrates and the spirit keeps on going.

OW: I haven't witnessed that yet, Julius.

Dr. Chepko: I read this in some books, that's why . . .

Voice: Mrs. Worrall, I wonder if you or Mr. Worrall have ever had an experience such as my friend, Dr. Osis, who was here in this group in a previous session, described, concerning people who are about to die—that they have a visitation from a friend or a relative or some unknown person at the time and it was seen by others also. Have you had experiences of that nature?

OW: Yes, I have.

Voice: How do you interpret it?

OW: They are waiting for the soul, for the person to come to the spiritual home. I had such an experience with a woman in our neighborhood who was stricken with cancer. I went to the home to make a

1. Doctor of Medicine; in general practice in Westminster, Md.

social call. I entered the bedroom alone, it was very pathetic, the members of the family were afraid to go into the room; they were so distressed. As I neared the bed I saw the sick woman's deceased mother sitting in the rocking chair. . . . I said to her, "Why don't you go away. . . ." But the mother said to me, "It's time for her to come. We're waiting for her."

Dr. Laidlaw: She was sitting in a physical rocking chair?

OW: She was sitting in the physical rocking chair . . . and I saw her in her astral body. My ill neighbor said to me, "You know it's the funniest thing. I don't know whether it's my imagination, but that chair keeps rocking."

But because Olga knew, she did not tell her what it was.

On the issue of how the astral body concept can or cannot be reconciled with the idea of reincarnation, the Worralls in their discussions revealed serious reservations. Neither denounced the theory of reincarnation; at the same time they clearly refused to accept the idea of the "shell" of a soul wandering lost and unhoused, so to speak, waiting for a return.

A part of one segment of dialogue illustrates their difficulty in making a direct or meaningful conformation between reincarnation as generally understood and their own psychic experiences:

Dr. Gardner: Mrs. Worrall, do these experiences of yours tend to cross out in your mind the idea of reincarnation?

OW: I can't accept reincarnation as it is currently presented. I know of people who lived on earth long ago and have communicated with them in the spirit world. Not once have I ever been told by a spirit that he had ever experienced reincarnation.

Dr. Gardner: I mean reincarnation in the Buddhist sense—multiple materializations.

AW: While we were being interviewed by listeners on a radio show the question was asked: "What do you know about reincarnation?" And I said, "I will give you my theoretical impression of what I think reincarnation is. I believe that everything that is created returns eventually to the source from which it came. Now, how long this takes I don't know. It may take ten thousand years; it may take one hundred thousand, ten million, or ten billion years. I don't know, but I believe that eventually every human soul will develop to the point where it no longer recognizes its separateness, that which weans it from the rest of the world, and will recognize itself in the other fellow to the extent that it is reabsorbed into that Being of no dimensions which we call God."

To me, this kind of reincarnation appeals logically, but to say that when a person dies his spiritual body is nothing but a shell which exists for varying periods, depending on who's talking: some say twenty years, some say one thousand and so on; that this shell is floating around in the atmosphere and that it can give information from its memory, I don't think that is true. We have received information that was not available at the time of death, but referred to future events which eventually came to pass.

It doesn't appeal to me because I'm speaking as someone who has had experiences in this other realm. I've had experience with clairvoyance, clairaudience, and what one man called mind travel.

One excerpt touched with unusual emphasis on the very diversity of values and questions about the ethereal plane, about the astral body and the physical, about reincarnation—the diverse nature of uncertainty itself. At one point, Olga had just spoken of astral travel while the physical body sleeps:

OW: . . . and I wakened.

Q: How do you distinguish that from the ordinary dream?

OW: Oh, you can tell.

Q: How?

OW: Unless you've experienced it yourself it is very difficult. When you have the experiences of a dream, you know it's a dream and you pay absolutely no attention to it because it is a dream. Something within you knows it's a dream, but when you have had the psychic experience, you awaken with the understanding that this was not just another dream.

AW: We have both traveled in the spiritual realm . . .

OW: Together . . .

AW: And I know from experience that you can see at a distance. Clairvoyantly you can see something taking place over in California. But you can also travel in your spirit and be there and see it. Now you can say, "How do you know that you are not seeing it clairvoyantly?" You know because you feel that you are there. You know you are right there in the room.

Dr. Laidlaw: You know that you are out of your body?

OW: That's right, and when you've seen yourself coming into your physical body . . . you see your body lying on the bed. . . .

I do want to add this experience that will help explain, in a way, why I do not accept the theory of reincarnation. Ambrose was asked to give healing to a child. The parents brought the little girl and her sister to our home. While one sister was taken upstairs into the healing room, the other sister stayed downstairs with her daddy and me. The father informed me that the child was an infant prodigy. . . . She was able to play the piano without having had piano lessons. The father asked the child to play something for me. I placed the child on the piano stool, and in the process of so doing I saw an elderly man in her aura. When the little girl placed her hands on the keys of the piano, I put my hands over them and I felt the hands of an old man. . . . Intuitively I received the message to the effect that when the child reached the age of about eight she would no longer respond to the influence of the controlling spirit, and would lose the ability to play the piano. As diplomatically as possible, I suggested to the father the advisability of sending the girl to the music conservatory for instructions. It would have been very disturbing to the parents to be told that their little girl was under the influence of a pianist who once lived on earth.

The sister who had need of Ambrose's healing ministry was restored to health, and from then on we saw nothing more of the family until . . . twelve years later when I was teaching in high school. It was the beginning of a new semester, and I was looking over the new class roll when my eye caught a name that sounded familiar to me. When the class assembled I asked the girl to come to my desk. I inquired if the girl's father had ever worked at a certain place of business. She informed me that he had, and then, seeing my name on the blackboard, she said, "Oh, Mrs. Worrall, my parents and my sister and I visited your home once, and my parents told us how Mr. Worrall was able

to heal my sister." "By the way," I said, "do you still play the piano?"
. . . She informed me that she hated it and added, "When I am sixteen
years old . . . I will no longer take piano lessons. I have only a few more
months to go before I reach that magic age, and then I will refuse to
touch that old piano again." I said, "That's strange, when did you
decide that you didn't like to play the piano?" Her answer was: "When
I was almost nine years old."

Dr. Laidlaw: But this was not reincarnation. This was possession.

OW: This is true; however, some members of the family and
friends were toying with the idea that the child was the reincarnation of
some great musician because of her amazing musical ability at such an
early age.

AW: We have not had any experiences that would justify the
belief in reincarnation.

Reincarnated—or astral?

It is one of the challenging questions in the modern world's exploration of psychic fields and the possibilities of what lies beyond
this waystop of reality.

6
A Time for Silence

The silence of which the psychic speaks is not the merely physical absence of external sound—nor even the extreme quiet of what is called the anechoic chamber, a solidly materialistic room which absorbs all sound external to the body. Psychic silence is of the spirit; it is the silence in which and through which the individual makes contact with other forces of the universe. It is the silence in which the mystic touches the hem of the infinite, the silence in which the pious Quaker and the Presbyterian alone in his hard-backed pew wait upon the Lord.

Silence of this kind is a listening, a waiting, and a reaching out; it is a telepathic pattern of paths and open lines that can carry the individual closer to the knowing, the understanding, the essence. It is the silence in which the healer transmits healing to the sick, in which the Capuchin monk, alone in his cell, communes. It is the quiet hour for you and God.

In the Worrall's book, *The Gift of Healing*, Ambrose declares, "In the silence I seek attunement with the patient. His spirit and my spirit are part of the universal, and I seek to harmonize them, to merge them completely. Spiritual being reaches out to spiritual being."

This silence as a force field in itself, a technique, an avenue, is available to all who learn to use it, to understand and practice it, to develop their own ability to reach beyond the clatter of the mundane—to reach first to the silence of the self and then to that of the spirit, the breath of divine force that is the ultimate reality.

Whatever our state of development, whatever level we have attained or seek to attain in understanding, this silence of which the psychic speaks is where true knowledge and insight begins, as spiritual discipline becomes truly purposeful. For the silence speaks in other ways than the physical. The stillness brings us to another level.

Ambrose's own statement, as the group began a probing with the Worralls into the dimension of spiritual silence, sharply outlined his perspective:

When we talk about sound, we are aware that there has to be an individual or there is no sound. If a person shuts out all sound, it doesn't exist for him even though it might be pounding in his ears. It's very difficult to find a quiet place these days. To go into the silence, we have to find some other method. You just can't get into an anechoic chamber unless you can rent one from the Bell Telephone Company. So we have to find another way.

Complete silence would be disturbing to some people, for it is a condition outside of their conscious experience. It is necessary that one withdrawing from sound be prepared to experience the silence that can be *felt*. If a person is afraid to be completely alone and lacks the courage to face the unknown, he is not prepared to seek silence.

In common with all other created things, we came out of the silence into the universe of sound. We came out of a state of perfect equilibrium, peace and unity, the static condition of cosmic being, and entered the realm of dynamic change, with its complexities, misunderstandings, and confusion. In a way, seeking silence is an attempt to return to the point of the beginning and look across the threshold into the anechoic chamber of pure ideas, to be consciously aware of perfection, to view reality, to experience divine order, and to receive wisdom.

The purpose of this exercise is to learn the nature of our native talents, to discover our spiritual gifts, to increase our understanding of creative law, to receive direction, to be restored, to obtain knowledge, to gain assurance which leads to self-confidence, to strengthen our intellectual belief and raise it to the level of a faith that can remove mountains, to prepare ourselves for wider service, to increase the affinity between ourselves and goodness, to develop our awareness of God.

Silence is greater than sound; all sound came out of silence. The vast nobility, grandeur, power, and beauty of the silence inspires awe, wonder and reverence. . . . Silence is to sound what contraterrene matter is to the material world, a necessary but illusive companion. Silence is vital to our study of spiritual healing. We must try to understand its reality and its nearness, for out of the silence comes the power that heals.

Learning to listen to the silence of which he speaks is not simple. The neophyte may close all doors and windows and find nonetheless an abundance of noise; the hubbub of his own thoughts resembles the cocktail hour; the problems of today or yesterday or tomorrow, the arguments won or lost, buzz and whirl in his mind.

Learning to know the difference between the clutter of our own personal thoughts, conscious and subconscious, and the impulses of the infinite that throb in the silence, is one of the first steps open to us in the learning process, the spiritual maturing.

Among parapsychologists, psychiatrists, and physicians, there is here, as in other fields of investigation, often a divergence of views. Are we speaking of physical silence or, actually, a spiritual, psychic force?

Do we really go from the physical to the spiritual and cosmic silence—or is what happens only an emotional reaction in which our awareness of silence operates merely as the opposite of our physical reaction to sound, as exemplified, for one instance, in the almost tangible silence of a pause between two segments of a composition by Debussy?

To Olga, spiritual silence, the quiet that grows in the supernormal, comes in the moments of clairvoyance:

OW: When you are receiving clairvoyantly, you automatically shut out sound. You shut out people around you; for a moment you are in complete silence. That is when you are perceiving on a higher level.

Just as, standing next to you, I suddenly became insensitive to everything going on around the room and I was able to perceive in that moment of silence.

Dr. Laidlaw: Just let me say—I know this group will be interested—Olga perceived with just pinpoint accuracy a clinical problem that I've been coping with all through last night and today, until I came here, without my having said anything to her at all—and giving me not only the essence of the case but what to do about it. This is the sort of thing that Eileen Garrett did with me some years ago in the some unerring way, and Olga has really been a big help to me today.

OW: Yes, I wanted to bring out that point. You instantly go into that silence that Ambrose has been talking about. You can't receive direction, you can't receive the information or guidance unless you are momentarily silent. Silence . . . is shutting out the material world. . . .

Dr. Osis: How does one train oneself to becoming aware inside? Maharishi called it the eloquence of silence and I suspect that what you both meant is not just keeping your mouth shut. It's something entirely different. What do you actually do? What is the training method?

OW: . . . I'm not a good one to tell you how to do it. I can only tell what I experience, but with me going into the silence is automatic when there is a need.

Mr. Laurance: I'd like to question the term "silence" the way you've been using it, because I think your description says not that you are going through a period of silence but that you are in a situation in which you have silenced one sphere in order to see more clearly another sphere. You're cutting out one portion in order to have a better reception. . . .

AW: You're tuning in on a different frequency.

OW: That's it, but for the moment I am not aware of this at all. The only way I could describe it in my unscientific way would be to say, "I'm listening to the other dimension."

Voice: Some people call it shifting of level or diminishing of consciousness. Would that be an accurate description?

AW: Yes, it's a good description.

Dr. Puharich: How would it be in an anechoic chamber, just as an example. Have you been in one, Ambrose?

AW: No, I've never been in one.

Dr. Puharich: Have you been in something similar to an anechoic chamber?

Voice: What is anechoic, anyway?

Dr. Puharich: It would probably be just the reverse because the environmental situation, which your body and ears are used to, would be removed and that would call attention to this and so it would take you away from this other thing . . . this silence you are speaking of.

Dr. Laidlaw: Is that the thing which you had in Maine, Andrija?

Dr. Puharich: No, an anechoic chamber is a room which absorbs all sound. If you say "Boo," it just gets absorbed in the walls. What you become aware of . . . I've been in the Bell Telephone anechoic room. You live in a world of external noise normally and you're never aware of internal noise, then suddenly you get in an anechoic chamber and you hear all kinds of squeaks and rumbles and bubbles inside of you. The internal noise, which is always there of course, suddenly becomes prominent. That's one thing you notice when you're in the middle of the desert. You hear your blood circulating and pounding and all these things that you don't hear at all usually.

Now you wouldn't be talking about that kind of silence? There's another kind of silence. I remember an associate of mine did an EEG study[1] on a couple of Yogins and he'd say, "Go into samadhi," and they'd go into samadhi and he found out that in this subjective state, which was self-induced, all the noise, the electrical noise of the EEG, died down and you had only a pure alpha rhythm. This was run through a computer analysis and found to be pure sine wave. They could switch it off and could do it with their eyes wide open or closed.

AW: When we go into this condition we're not aware of our physical bodies. When I'm doing healing I'm not aware of my physical body. I know it's there, it's more like a shadow; I'm not conscious of its weight, for instance.

Dr. Puharich: Suppose you went into a session and you happened to have some ache or pain somewhere, would that . . . ?

OW: That would vanish.

---

1. This refers to the electroencephalograph, a machine that measures nerve impulses from the brain.—W.O.

Dr. Puharich: Do you think you get some sense of dissociation, stepping out of your body?

AW: When I'm treating by the laying-on-of-hands, it feels as though there's a separation of maybe a quarter of an inch from the person. I've always thought that, although my physical hand was resting on the person, I was actually feeling with my spiritual body and that this was giving the sense of being a quarter of an inch away. However, there could be another explanation. The etheric double, as they call it, is slightly larger than the physical body because it has emanations and, possibly, when I put my hand on the physical body, I actually feel the etheric double. I'm not sure what happens. All I know is I have the sensation of my hand being perhaps a quarter of an inch away from the body.

Dr. Puharich: Do you have any problem when you are in that state, of remembering what goes on?

AW: Yes. I don't remember most of the time.

In a modern English translation of the book *Tao-teh-king*, one reads: "Whoever knows does not speak; whoever speaks does not know. So, stop the senses. Close their doors. Solve their riddles. Subdue their light. Be one with humble dust. This is the mystic unity."

The silence of which the mystics speak is a glimpse of the path that leads to the opening of the true self to the self, the opening of the skies in all their magnificence.

Silence in this sense is a journey that we enter upon; to reach our goals here we must learn to get past the barriers and obstacles and detours brought on by a myriad of external forces. Yet it cannot be a drugged thing nor a hypnotic thing. True silence is a full awareness of the total Self in its relationship to the total Other, to what Martin Buber calls the I and Thou, or—to use a different image— it is the relationship of the finite and immediate with the infinite and eternal.

The layman who seeks such a path encounters enormous obstacles. The world is so much with us; there are so many noises to torment and torture, to blast and blare; the soul grows weary to the point of almost total capitulation to the roaring assault of modern materiality. This assault is the counterforce as pictured by Ambrose; it is the invading destroyer:

> We are all aware of the effect of external stimuli upon the mind. Advertising, of course, is a demonstration of the effect of external stimuli upon people. People are impressed to go out and buy things which they don't need, because they had it shown to them in the proper way to stimulate them to go out and make the purchase. So we are all affected by external stimuli which come through the five senses.
>
> Psychosomatic illness, of course, is well demonstrated these days, and much of this comes from external stimuli which affect the level of the mind below the waking consciousness. Well, we humans store a lot of satellites in the subconscious. We are responsible for putting many of them into orbit. Some of them we have a little difficulty in shooting down before we find out we should never have started them in the first place.
>
> This is what they call clutter in outer space—clutter in the mind. These satellites, which are in orbit in our minds, beam back thoughts to the conscious level of mind and, if allowed, can make us slaves. . . .

The Worralls speak of another kind of silence, that which Ambrose describes as *silentium altum*—deep silence. This involves not only the elimination of external stimuli but also a deliberate withdrawal from physical self and environment, through the process of meditation and contemplation, lifting the mind and the ideals into the realm of pure mind and pure thought. It is a process of tuning the mind to the wave lengths beyond any possible material range. We catch vibrations of this metaphysical wave length in the brief but almost overpowering Biblical words, "Be still and know that I am God. . . ."

Ambrose in his pamphlet, *Silentium Altum*—the pamphlet was part of the orientation of those at the seminars—describes some of the ways by which the individual can begin to achieve the level of deep silence:

Thought control starts with selective thinking. If there is a thought that should be avoided do not entertain it. Some have tried to destroy thoughts by fighting them. This is not a successful method. The way to overcome unwanted thought is to think its opposite. In this way hope replaces despair, confidence replaces fear, success takes the place of failure and faith takes the place of doubt.

Practicing selective thinking makes the mind responsive to the selected level of thought subjects. Other levels of thought do not make impressions because the mind is not responsive to their particular frequencies.

To Ambrose the deep silence is an achieving of the most profound level of union between the living, physical being and the cosmic. It is when he has entered the deep silence that the person becomes aware of what is called the Presence—the Holy Spirit. He declares in *Silentium Altum*:

In the deep silence it is possible to have revelations. These seem to have no relation to time as we know it. It is as though one suddenly becomes aware of something that had been buried deep in the consciousness. As far as the earth is concerned it may belong to the future, but in the state of deep silence time does not exist, and that which is revealed out of time will surely come to pass when time is fitted into the equation.

Occasionally experiences in deep silence may be of such a nature that they can only be understood under the conditions that pertain to deep silence, and there are no means of conveying this experience or its meaning to the temporal world. This knowledge thus gained is of enlightenment only to the one thus blessed. The world is not ready for it, and cannot receive it.

Achievement of this state demands the uttermost in spiritual discipline. It is given only to a few. For those who would dare to make the try, the silent path here has been described by Ambrose in one of his other pamphlets, entitled *Meditation and Contemplation*, in these words:

> Contemplation . . . is reaching through meditation to higher ground, the reaching of a state of rapt regard for creation. It finds in one idea, on which attention is concentrated, the divine essence in every quality and aspect. It is an overflowing awareness of all creation.
>
> Thus, beginning with meditation, an attempt to reach the reality of God by reaching out for the Kingdom within ourselves, the seeker after spiritual truth progresses to contemplation. The material world, even his own body, becomes unreal as he rises to an intuitive consciousness of the Divine Reality. From here, continuing in contemplation and ever alert for further knowledge, the seeker becomes more and more aware of his affinity with God until at last he realizes that all are one and that God is in every part of his own being.

7
Force Fields of Healing

Life, Ambrose states, is God expressing himself through creation. But life and creation are not confined only to visible or physical reality but are equally part of the ethereal.

Further, the creativity of which he speaks applies especially to healing, to making people whole, instantly, by the application of creative regenerative force—the ultimate source of which is the healing will of God.

This healing force Ambrose views in some cases as a creativity in reverse because while in one situation a tumor or other abnormal growth may shrink or totally disappear, in another a shriveled leg or arm may grow back to full restoration.

In response to a question from one doctor at the seminar, Ambrose described how this creative force functions through the psychic healer:

Q: I would like to address myself to one point you mentioned—this process of creation in reverse with respect to healing. Of course you said we didn't know in the physical world how matter was created or destroyed. Actually we're still seeking an answer. From a practical point of view, will you tell us what you have personally seen, what you mean by this?

AW: Let me give you this example: We had a girl about fifteen years old who had been injured at birth. The mother had a convulsion when the child was being born and, from what I understand, in this convulsion she crushed the back of the skull into the brain. The child grew up with the left side of her body very much underdeveloped. The limbs were the same length, but the left leg was approximately half the diameter of the right leg and the left arm just hung by her side. She never used it. The ribs, of course, were underdeveloped also; and they doctored her . . . from birth on. An examination by a brain specialist revealed that an operation to relieve this condition would probably be fatal and he advised against it, so the parents came to accept it as a condition they could do nothing about. The child had convulsions all the time, and when she became old enough to menstruate she didn't menstruate, and every time the period time came along she would get into a terrible emotional state; she couldn't hold her water, and when she tried to talk she didn't have proper control of her jaw and her teeth would chatter. She would try to say something and would finally say, "Oh, skip it." But, her mind was working all right; she was quite an intelligent girl. I worked with this girl for three years, two hundred hours I worked on her with my hands, and gradually things started to take place. After two weeks, she had a normal menstrual period and then in about a month or six weeks she was able to control her bladder, and gradually the arm started to come back to life, the ribs started to fill out, the leg got fatter.

I was seeing her three times a week for the first year and twice a week for the second year and by that time she was able to go back to school—previously they wouldn't let her go to school because she was a disturbing influence. She went back to school. Her arm had come back to life so she could learn to type. In the third year I saw her only once a week, and at the end of the third year both sides were completely balanced and she was a normal beautiful girl. She later got married and is now a grandmother. She never had any return of the condition.

I look upon that as a kind of form of creation. How that skull was brought back out of the brain I don't know, or whether it was actually brought back out of the brain, but anyway all the problems disappeared and the doctor said, "I don't know what you're doing but you keep right on doing it."

Spiritual healers frequently declare that they do not do the healing, God does. Yet some people, like the Worralls, do appear to have a gift for healing, where others do not. Part of the objective of the seminars was to seek deeper understanding of how spiritual healing actually functions, by what psychic-mystical means spiritual intervention occurs. To Ambrose the *modus operandi* is both mystical and religious in character; it is the acceptance of God as the reality, the Universal Mind. It is the acceptance also of the mystical plane—including our own physical lives and needs—as part of the Universal Mind and concern:

AW: The Universal Mind contains . . . every imaginable problem with the answer to each problem; and man's desire selects one particular idea from this Universal Mind to suit his purpose. He gives it motion by applying his will, and the perfect law governing the direction and extent of the motion brings forth a perceivable manifestation. *This principle of mind is important in the understanding of how spiritual healing works.*

We read in the 27th verse of the first chapter of Genesis: "So God created man in his own image, in the image of God created he him." Within every man is that which is God's image. The physical body of man is not God's image. It, like all other perceptible phenomena, is a manifestation of God's perfect law. God's image is without form and void; it is the same in man as in God himself. It is not until the Spirit of God moves upon the image that we have the form we call man. In the second chapter of Genesis in the seventh verse, this "Spirit of God" is called the "breath of life." This is what is said: "And the Lord God formed man of the dust of the ground, and breathed into his nostrils the breath of life; and man became a living soul." Most people cannot understand how this would be possible.

Let's change the picture a little and make it more understandable. We'll think not of the dust of the earth and the material body formed from it in the shape of a man, but of a spiritual body that evolved in a spiritual environment as the Will of God brought motion to bear on his idea of man. Man became manifest as a living soul, later to be clothed in material particles made from the "dust" of the earth with a lot of water added.

As Paul the Apostle said in his First Epistle to the Corinthians, chapter 15, verse 44: "There is a natural body, and there is a spiritual body." *The existence of the spiritual body is an important principle involved in spiritual healing.* We have to keep that in mind. . . .

The action patterns of the force are still largely unknown variables. There are times when the force works or appears to work on the individual and times when it does not, even with the ministrations of science and effective psychic healers. Moreover, with the objective consideration of the seminars, it is difficult to move from the empirical healing or change in physical condition, which can be positively observed and recorded, to the causal forces behind these changes. It is also difficult to explain why these channels of divine healing are apparently open and effective in one case—but in another appear to be closed and ineffective.

Challenging also is the question of why in paranormal therapy something totally unexpected and unlooked for—even by the healer —may take place:

AW: There is only one case in my healing experience which approaches anything like psychic surgery, and that concerned a little girl twelve years old whom I was actually treating for St. Vitus's dance. She had a cyst on her eye about the size of a grape which doctors were afraid would affect her eyesight. The surgeons said they could not operate because they were afraid she would have a convulsion when they were operating. They told the parents that the St. Vitus's dance must be cured first and then they could take the cyst off.

The girl's father asked me if I would be able to help her. When she came for treatment I found three cysts on her leg. I said to her father, "Did you know she had these?" He said, "No, I didn't know." She said, "Daddy, I've had those for years." They were like peas in size. I had the impression just to hold one in my fingers. I was holding it in my fingers, while I was talking to her father, and suddenly I felt something pop and I looked in my hand and I had this cyst (or whatever it was—it was a lump, like a pea). I looked down at her leg and there wasn't any sign of a mark. I gave the cyst to her father and said, "You can have this for a souvenir." I took hold of the second one and that, too, popped into my hand. I took hold of the third one and, by this time, I was fully confident that this was going to happen every time. Nothing happened to the third one at this time. After a number of treatments the St. Vitus's dance disappeared, so did the cyst under the eye, and the third cyst from her leg. I think this is a very interesting case: Why would two of these cysts be removed from her leg as though excised by some sort of surgery which left no marks, while the other cysts were caused to slowly disappear over a period of time?

Dr. Puharich: There was no mark left?

AW: Absolutely no mark. . . .

Dr. Laidlaw: This would have had to be a dematerialization, then a rematerialization, an apport of a type.

OW: It was apported off the body . . . dematerialized.

AW: The peculiar thing about this is that I didn't do anything myself. I was just holding a conversation with the child's father when it happened. I wasn't thinking or willing the cysts away, or anything like that; there must be some kind of force at work . . . with an intelligence behind it, controlling it. Some day I hope to find out what it is. . . .

In healing that involves dissolution, the dissolving of a condition, the usual cases are, of course, tumors.

I administered healing to two ladies; one was from the church where we have healing services. She had had an operation on one breast and she was ready to go in for an operation on the other for removal of a lump, when Dr. Robert G. Kirkley, the minister and Director of the New Life Clinic at the Mount Washington United Methodist Church, said, "Before you go to the hospital, why don't you try Mr. Worrall." He sent her over to our home. I held the lump in my fingers and in fifteen minutes it was gone.

In the same month I administered healing to the other lady; her letter describing the case is included in our book, *The Gift of Healing*. She also had a lump in her breast and had been to three different physicians, all of whom told her she had to go to the hospital. With this lady it took about four treatments before the lump disappeared.

What I want to point out here is that the lady from the church was the outgoing extrovert while the other lady was the introvert, very shy and retiring. Perhaps their different mental attitudes had something to do with the length of time required to effect a cure. In both cases the lumps have not returned.

Not all are healed; some are not even helped. Yet the Worralls estimate that 90 per cent who come to their home asking for help are aided, and as many as 50 to 60 per cent are made well. Whether the illness or disablement was organic, functional, or psychosomatic is a question the Worralls leave to the physicians. They themselves are not medical practitioners in any sense. Further, they do not take people who have refused to have medical examination and care.*

One of the problems in evaluation of healings by percentages is that so many cases come to Olga and Ambrose after the physicians have given up any hope of healing or helping the patient. Olga herself, in fact, had a growth on her hand which the doctors had tried without success to get rid of. Ambrose had held her wrist a number of times without any effect.

Finally, the pain of this growth became almost too great:

OW: On this particular night it was so painful I kept bargaining with God. I'd say, "Please God, let it go away, but don't let it go any place else." You know, I didn't want it under cover. I wanted it where I could see it. Finally, I just couldn't stand it any longer and I said, "O God, please heal my wrist." And a voice just as distinct as yours said to me, "Ask Ambrose to put his hand on it." Ambrose was half asleep, so I nudged my good husband and I said, "Sweetheart, put your hand on my wrist—it hurts me—and heal it." Half asleep, he said, "I've been waiting for you to ask me." He put his hand on my wrist and promptly fell fast asleep.

In the morning I was in a big hurry to get him off to work, and I walked out to the garage with him to close the garage doors. When I walked back, my next-door neighbor who was hanging out her wash stopped to speak with me. After a moment she said, "Oh, I see you had

* As this book goes to press the Worralls have announced their semi-retirement. They no longer give individual treatments in their home but are continuing their daily 9:00 P.M. silent prayer healing ministry.

that terrible lump removed." I looked down at my wrist and saw that the lump was gone. I just said, "Yes, it's gone." I could barely make it into the kitchen. I sat on the stool and I sobbed, I was so shaken with what I witnessed, thanking God all the while. That night when Ambrose came home from work I said, "Sweetheart, it's gone." He looked at my healed wrist and I can tell you his eyes were filled with tears too.

AW: I think the healer has better luck, as I have noted before, if he just gets himself out of the way—in this case, by my going to sleep.

Dr. Laidlaw: Ambrose, was that case which illustrated dematerialization and rematerialization unique in your experience, or have you had others where pathological matter has suddenly appeared in your hand?

AW: The only case was the case of the little girl and the cysts. Usually as with a tumor, it just melts and disappears.

Dr. Robert Shaw:[1] What percentage of the people whom you try to help respond to your treatment?

AW: I don't have any percentages because a large percentage of our work is done without seeing people, with absent treatment. You may not hear for two years about a case that was healed and perhaps you will never hear about it. Usually we hear when a person who was helped or healed is asking help for someone else.

OW: I think Dr. Shaw is asking about people that have actually come to the home. Of the people who came—now I'm using this figuratively—I would say that the majority of the people who have come to us have been helped or healed. The others have come to us when they were in terminal stages of disease, when the body was so badly diseased that it did not respond to healing treatment.

Dr. Shaw: Have you had experience with people with terminal cancer, who were in great pain and difficulty, in making them more comfortable?

OW: Yes, this is really very mysterious. So often people have called saying that some loved one is in terrible pain and asking us to pray for relief for the person. We hold the person in prayer. I always hold the thought that God grant that their remaining days be days of comfort and freedom from pain. Frequently the pain disappears and

1. Doctor of medicine; vascular surgeon, Massachusetts General Hospital.

drugs are no longer needed to relieve pain. How is your father doing, Andrija?

Dr. Puharich: I'll tell you . . . Bob [addressing Dr. Shaw], you know my father, but you haven't seen him as he's in the hospital desperately ill with terminal cancer. I asked the Worralls, about four and a half months ago, the very same thing. Dad's spine, pelvic bone, is just riddled. His bladder is loaded. He bleeds a half pint of blood a day or more—a tremendous amount of bleeding—the whole problem of cancer in the terminal stage, and he has never asked for Demerol or morphine. He's had no narcotics. I've never seen one that far advanced so free from pain. Incidentally, I've never told my father that I made this request for relief from pain to the Worralls. He's an old skeptic and doesn't believe in anything to do with faith healing.

OW: He doesn't have to know. It will interest you to know that doctors who know us call us and say, "I've got a patient who is in the last stages of cancer. Will you and Ambrose hold him in prayer so he won't suffer." Something happens; the patient is not healed of cancer but is relieved of the pain. Then the doctors will call and say, "Thanks, Olga, it has resulted in a peaceful ending; the patient was free from pain and just closed his eyes."

AW: This relieving of pain, of course, is a little different when the person doesn't know about it than when the person does know about it. Probably the best illustration I have of this is the case of a girl whom I had treated for tuberculosis. When she was nine years old, I treated her and she got well very rapidly.

This girl apparently had great faith in me. Later she got married and moved to a distant city. When it was time for her child to be born she told her husband to telephone me and to "tell Uncle Ambrose that I'm going to have my baby and to send me some help." I told her husband to go back and tell her to relax and I would take care of her. When the doctor asked her how she felt, she said, "All I feel is something pushing down." She gave birth to the baby without pain.

Dr. Shaw: One of the most tragic things to see is advanced rheumatoid arthritis. Have you had any experience with that?

OW: Yes, we have a woman who comes to us to the New Life Clinic. She came to us on crutches and had to be assisted up the steps to the sanctuary. She's been coming to us for a year. She now walks without crutches. It was in her joints and knuckles. It is gradually diminishing and she is now able to use her hands.

Dr. Shaw: And without pain?

OW: Yes, without pain. But, of course, we can't say that everybody who would come to us would be healed, but she has responded well to treatment.

Of particular importance to doctors at the seminars were descriptions of actual various methods of paranormal healing as carried out by the healer. Neither of the Worralls can say precisely from where came their spiritual gift; both agree that it can be developed, but it is clear that the gift, like any talent, is special and individual and easier to develop in one person than in another.

One method employed by both Olga and Ambrose is that of visualizing. This is important in cases of absent healing. Very often they will ask someone seeking help to send a picture so that the visualization can be as accurate as possible.

OW: In spiritual healing you do visualize. You are holding a thought for a person, you are seeing that particular organ being restored to perfection. Now, you were talking about the heart. Ambrose was asked to give healing to a little boy who had a very large hole in his heart . . .

AW: . . . the size of a quarter.

OW: He was born with this condition. The doctor said they would have to build the child up before they could perform open-heart surgery. The parents came to us and asked if Ambrose could do something to help the child. The child had blue lips and, of course, was very tired. Any little thing was an effort. Ambrose began to administer spiritual healing to that boy and within a few weeks the blueness left his lips; the child became energized and able to compete with all the kids in school. After a year they decided he was in such excellent condition that they could open the heart and see what they could do to mend the hole. The original test showed that the hole was about the size of a quarter. When they opened him up they found it was a very tiny . . .

AW: An eighth of an inch in diameter . . .

OW: . . . and they were able to do plastic surgery on the heart. But I think the interesting thing is that whenever we thought of that heart when we held it in healing, it was: "The heart is becoming perfect." I was visualizing the hole getting smaller.

One method frequently employed in this form of healing is the laying-on-of-hands, often carried out in conjunction with other methods, including prayer and, particularly in Roman Catholic healing, anointing with oil. The hands of the healer are extremely important. They often appear to have in them unusual heat. This writer on one occasion interviewed a man who claimed to have been healed of an extremely serious heart condition by Oral Roberts. When I asked what effect he experienced when Roberts put his hand on him, the man replied, "Mister, I'm an electrician. I know what an electric shock is like. Well—this was like an electric shock."

Other healers have a different effect, perhaps not dramatic in the excitement of the experience but equally real and equally strong. The heat of the healing hand is often noted by the patient. There is also a sense of the warmth of the whole person, the community of being, not physically, but spiritually, psychically.

Declared Ambrose of this role of the healing hands in psychic therapy:

AW: It is interesting to note that in the practice of the laying-on-of-hands in spiritual healing therapy, it is a common practice for the healer to place his hands on the patient's head. I'm a little different. I put them almost anywhere.

Several questions are raised as we examine this practice. One current is already flowing in the patient's head and another in the healer's hands. What happens upon physical contact of the healer's hands with the patient's head? Joining of two conductors can have several effects on the current flow in both circuits. Differences in potentials, the direction of current flow, and the manner in which the two circuits are joined must be taken into account.

It is possible that entirely different results may be obtained for different positioning of the healer's hands with respect to the patient's head. The practice of some healers is to follow a standard routine of placing their hands in approximately the same position, on the heads of all patients treated. Sometimes this is mere force of habit, at other times it is physically most convenient. Then, of course, it may be looked upon as the conventional and approved manner of administering this form of spiritual therapy. Some other points may be raised. Should the hands of a left-handed healer be placed in the same position, all other things being equal, on the head of a left-handed patient as on the head of a right-handed patient? Should the hands of a female healer be placed in the same position on a male patient's head as on the head of a female patient?

Things become even more complex when the healer treats two patients at the same time, his left hand being placed on the head of the patient to his left, and his right hand on the patient to his right. I was thinking particularly of Dr. Price[2] of Philadelphia. In this type of therapy the patients are usually kneeling at a rail and in contact with each other. The practice of loading the rail to full capacity sometimes places the whole group of patients in contact like the links of a chain. Beneficial effects have been reported under the several methods used in the laying-on-of-hands. In those cases where the healer has spiritual discernment or receives spiritual guidance as to the manner in which his hands should be applied to the patient, an additional factor is added, the significance of which may be a matter of opinion, but it requires consideration.

When you register these impressions, it is different from clairvoyance, where you actually see what is wrong. A clairvoyant may see that the aura is drooping in a certain area and she knows something is wrong because the life emanations are not standing out at ninety degrees from the body as they ought to be in health. It's also different from a healing voice that tells you what is wrong. That is clairaudience. These other sensations are classified under the term clairsentience, clear feeling.

There's the possibility that when the spiritual healer applies his hands to the patient, the atomic thermal pattern is changed and the

2. Dr. Alfred W. Price, well-known healing minister of St. Stephen's Episcopal Church in Philadelphia.

disorder disappears. Now this may occur only when the hands of the healer are correctly applied. It is evident, from the high percentage of failures to obtain results, that a standard method of the laying-on-of-hands with all patients is a questionable procedure. Science could some-day determine the atomic thermal patterns of health for every organ in the human body, and the means of determining any departure there-from. And I would not rule out the possibility of the development of an apparatus capable of changing these atomic thermal patterns to restore health. In this way, mechanical healers may do the equivalent of the laying-on-of-hands in the doctor's office or in a hospital. I'll just leave this thought with you as a possible starting point of some future re-search. After all they wouldn't believe in clairvoyance so they developed the X-ray machine, so they had a mechanical clairvoyant that could see inside the body.

We can conceive of a healthy organ as one containing no con-taminating material and being the correct size and shape for perfect health. This healthy organ has atomic thermal patterns that produce inaudible sound vibrations which blend in a symphony of health. In the case of a sick organ, all that is necessary to restore it to health, it would seem, is to change its tune. . . . Could this be the way spiritual healing works?

For example, Dr. Day[3] had an enlarged heart. While attending a meeting in Washington he suffered a heart attack. A medical exam-ination and X rays disclosed an enlarged heart and a heart block. On this particular morning, a week after the heart attack, Dr. Day, prior to the healing service of the New Life Clinic, was sitting in prayer with Olga, his Associate, and the Associate's wife. Dr. Day's deceased mother appeared clairvoyantly to Olga and said, "We want you to put your hand over Albert's heart. . . ."

Olga, you tell the story. . . .

OW: I was at a loss to know how to approach Dr. Day with this message, since I had not known him long enough to appreciate just how he would accept a clairvoyant message that involved his deceased mother

3. Dr. Albert E. Day, who retired in 1957, was the former minister and Director of the New Life Clinic at the Mt. Vernon Place Methodist Church in Baltimore.

and her desire that I act as a channel for the healing force. Dr. Day was sitting at his desk with his head resting on his arms. His mother gave me the following message: "You must place your hands on Albert's chest and back, we are ready to answer his prayer and heal him." My mental reply was that I could do no such thing. However, the mother, quite insistent, stated, "But you must!" After a few more moments of hestitation, I gathered up courage and said, "Dr. Day, your mother is here (I described her, giving her name and other personal details), she tells me that I must place my hands over your heart because they're ready to heal you."

He didn't hesitate. He lifted up his head and said, "By all means do as you feel guided." I placed one hand over the heart and one on the back. Instantly I felt a surge of energy go through my hands, and for the first time I realized the full implications of Jesus' remark when he stated he felt virtue leave him. Apparently Dr. Day felt something coming into his body, for immediately after I removed my hands he exclaimed, "That girl has healing in her hands. I felt something."

Later more tests were made and X rays taken. The result of these tests showed that the heart had returned to normal size and the heart block was no longer there.

Question: Also the electrocardiograph changed?

OW: Yes.

Q: There was a block—a heart block?

OW: Yes, a heart block and an enlarged heart, according to hospital tests made previously in Pasadena.

Like many others in healing, Ambrose and Olga are concerned as to the nature of the thermal factor in the healing hands—a phenomenon more familiar and frequent than the electrical charge some healers appear to have. The heat is generated to a level that can be felt even when the hands of the healer are held several inches or more away:

AW: It is possible that there may be a clue to the nature of these frequencies in the sensation of heat that seems to accompany the laying-on-of-hands, and this is not the same as the warmth of your hand. It's a different kind of heat. Patients feel it as though you had an electric pad upon their bodies. Now we know that in every degree of temperature above absolute zero there is thermal motion of the atom. Thermal motion and heat are synonymous. In other words, we think of heat as the motion of the atom. The patterns of thermal motion of the atoms in a living body are no doubt extremely complex. Science tells us that when there is heat, you will also have sound, for the two are inseparable. Now this may not be audible sound but nevertheless it acts like sound. Each atomic thermal pattern has its own peculiar sound and it broadcasts a series of tones that are characteristic of its substance and shape.

Dr. Walter Pahnke:[4] With regard to this heat that you were talking about, is that something that would be correlated with the amount of healing? I mean, does everyone feel some heat when you put your hands on them?

AW: The majority of people feel it.

Dr. Pahnke: If they felt it to an intense degree, would that mean that more force was probably being transmitted, and there would be more chance of healing?

AW: That is a possibility, even a probability.

Dr. Laidlaw: The interesting thing is a deep heat. When Eileen Garrett puts her hands . . . you feel it immediately about an inch below the surface of the skin.

AW: It's like a diathermy type of heat. It's not the usual heat.

Dr. Pahnke: How can you tell? Can you feel it in your hands?

AW: Yes, I feel it. To me it feels like warm air coming out of my hands. However, again, a healer can only explain what he feels. What he feels may be just the side effects. We must look to science to find out the true nature of the energies involved.

OW: Walter, sometimes when I put my hands on a person, the person will say, "I just feel something penetrating like an electric current, and it's hot, it's burning me." Again others will feel nothing unusual, yet they'll receive beneficial results. So, you can't always tell. If a person is not sensitive to the energy being transmitted he may not feel it, but I can feel it coming out of my hands.

4. Doctor of medicine; doctor of philosophy; psychiatrist; Chief of Psychiatric Research, Maryland Psychiatric Research Center, Baltimore.

AW: One lady whom Olga laid her hands on said the sensation was similar to what would be felt if a big corkscrew were turning inside her abdomen. That was the lady, mentioned in *The Gift of Healing*, that had the abdominal tumor about the size of your head. That was the way she felt the healing force. The tumor slowly reduced in size and in a few months no trace of it could be found.

Dr. Pahnke: Ambrose, you feel something like warm air coming from your hands. Olga, you don't feel it so much that way?

OW: It depends . . .

AW: I feel the electrical-like currents too.

OW: . . . like pins and needles. You have all touched a live wire at some time or other. You know the shock you get from it. That's what I feel in my hands.

AW: It's not as powerful as the sensation experienced when bridging 117v 60-cycle electrical supply lines!

OW: Oh no. But the prickly sensation is what is felt.

AW: It's as if you took the terminals of a battery and touched them to your tongue. We used to do that when we were children and referred to it as tasting the electricity. You get a little tingling sensation and that's what you often feel in your hands when you put them on a patient—but not always. It seems to vary in potential, but it makes me believe there is an electrical component involved in spiritual healing when doing the laying-on-of-hands.

Q: Hasn't anyone tried to pick this up?

AW: Wainwright House conducted an experiment along these lines. Julius Weinberger, an electronic scientist, devised the method used. A piece of dental X-ray film was placed on the palm of my hand with a lead bar across it, the whole apparatus was attached with adhesive tape. I asked, "What is that for?" Dr. Weinberger said, "You say you feel this force flowing down your arm and out of your hand, and we think it might build up against the lead bar and maybe it will show something on this film." There was an ill woman in the next room who had been brought in to participate in the experiment. Dr. Weinberger asked me to put my hand on her and tell him if I felt the power flowing. This I did. They took the X-ray film from my hand, developed it, and there appeared a line of light on the film where the bar had been. They made some checks which indicated that the line was not caused by X ray. I don't know whether or not they pursued it far enough to determine the nature of the energy involved, but I found out that it takes only a few electron volts to affect X-ray film. I hope to pursue this a little further with some of my scientific friends.

Prayer—especially affirming prayer—is considered one of the most powerful forces in all healing and is almost universally practiced by charismatic healers as a part of their participation in this form of therapy. However, over and over again, Olga and Ambrose warn that it is important for the healer, once he has carried out his ministrations, to "get out of the way" of the psychic process itself.

This getting out of the way allows the healing force to take over within the patient rather than the force field of any other person, even of the healer. Prayer is a force field of action and counteraction and so it must be used with great care, knowledge, and understanding. Healing techniques when misused—even inadvertently —can harm as well as help.

Ambrose in fact reported on what can happen when someone who may know a little but not enough about the varied techniques of prayer becomes involved in trying to heal:

Now, take the case of this little girl who was in the hospital. She had developed encephalitis after an attack of the measles. She was in a coma for sixteen days and the parents were told there was no history of recovery after a sixteen-day coma. I was asked to help. The girl's father provided me with a snapshot of the little girl for the purpose of concentration. This story is a good example of the interference that can be caused by a sincere desire on the part of a person to be helpful in promoting a healing, but who is unaware of the laws involved.

My first attempt to treat this child by the absent treatment method was not successful. I had not seen the patient, so I used her photograph for visualization. Entering into attunement with the child, I felt the energy flow from my solar plexus and travel in her direction. It seemed to reach a point within three feet of her body, but appeared unable to penetrate some force field that surrounded her. This was a new experience for me, and I sought information regarding the nature of this barrier to the healing power. Presently, the face of the child's father appeared to me clairvoyantly. I noted the deep concentration in his features, and realized that he had something to do with the creation of this unseen barrier between the healing force and his daughter.

The following morning, in answer to my questions, the father said that at the time that I was attempting to reach the child on the previous evening, he was concentrating on the child's paralyzed throat muscles, trying to make them relax (she was being fed through a tube inserted through her nose into her stomach). His intent was good, but his procedure was wrong, and did not have the results desired.

We decided to use a different procedure for the second attempt. The father was to think of the child as being in a perfect state of health. There was to be no thought of the disease, and no deep concentration, but rather a relaxed picturing of his daughter playing and running as in normal health. That night I repeated the effort of the previous night; the healing power flowed from my solar plexus; there was no opposing force field around the child, and she responded by opening her eyes and coming out of the coma. This was the eighteenth day of the coma.

In this case a change in the father's thinking had a profound effect upon the psychical conditions around his sick daughter, conditions that were important to the success of absent healing treatment. How one prays for the sick is a subject that must be given prime consideration. It can mean the difference between success and failure.

In this case absent treatment did not result in complete healing. Some weeks after the child was discharged from the hospital, her father asked me if I would visit her at home to see if she could be helped further. He told me the disease had left her with only 10 per cent eyesight and she was without the use of her legs from the waist down. Olga and I went to see the child. I felt impressed to make circular motions with my right hand in contact with her back, and she said it felt good. I did not tell the child she was receiving a spiritual healing treatment; she would not have understood. In all we spent about an hour with the child.

The next morning, to everyone's surprise, this little six-year-old girl was walking and running as though she had never been ill. Her vision returned to normal. Now in her late twenties, married and a mother, she reports no ill effects whatsoever from her bout with encephalitis.

Prayer can be many, many things, of course. Usually if you go to any spiritual healing service, the minister or priest prays. Some pray over the individual, some over pairs of individuals; others pray for the entire congregation. This brings in a factor we should probably look into. If we look upon prayer as directed thought, and accept the experimental evidence that thought transference is not conditioned by distance, then we might postulate that effects registered by a patient treated at a distance occur because of telepathic rapport or attunement between the source of the prayer and the patient. This premise would hold in all types of absent treatment—the single healer; the prayer group; or the church service. It would be very interesting to find out the operations that take place under these different conditions.

Both Olga and Ambrose know the fullness of prayer at work each evening at the nine o'clock silent prayer session. Their method, as Olga has described it, is not one of striving but of letting the forces with which they work emanate from them to those whom they hold in their thoughts, their love, their prayer.

Ambrose, in a paper on the healing methods which the Worralls use, and the theory behind it, sums up those methods in his own scientific-technical-spiritual blending of dimensions or forces at work:

> When the force fields of healer and patient are in harmonial relationship with each other they can be coupled by bringing the two together. The force fields immediately become as one producing a common vibratory field for both individuals. The result can be likened to multiple chords on an organ, but on an inaudible band of frequencies.
>
> The effect of this coupling is to amplify the weaker tones and to subdue the louder tones until the final result is one perfect chord, like the sound of a grand Amen. This is the balanced condition in which the healing power operates.

8
Possessed by What?

Various rituals, both contemporary and ancient, are employed to placate or exorcise entities—evil or otherwise—that assertedly have "possessed" an individual. Protestant and Roman Catholic churches alike have "exorcising" priests and pastors, trained in techniques of depossessing such uninvited entities. Over the centuries the invoking of such practice has not been limited merely to the superstitious, the illiterate, or so-called primitive peoples.

Underlying the surface of highly rationalistic ancient Greece was a flourishing belief in spirits and shamanistic practices. A kind of collective possession was exemplified in the frenzied rituals of Dionysiac religion. Even the priestesses at Delphi delivered oracular pronouncements in a state of supposed temporary possession by the god—although anthropologists believe they more likely inhaled fumes of some ancient form of cannabis.

Neither Olga nor Ambrose, as their reports to the seminars disclosed, treats possession as merely theoretical. Their claim is built out of individual personal experience and empirical results, the products of psychic intuition and second sight.

To both, the phenomenon of possession is as real as any physical or personality disorder. They see what they see; hear what they hear. To them there can be no challenge to the reality. For example, in the days of Jesus and, in fact, in some instances down to modern times, most cases of insanity were considered as being at least in part demon possession. In 1969, a young girl was beaten to death in Scotland in an effort of "kindly" neighbors to drive a possessing devil out of her. One notes, however, that while Jesus dealt with demon possession, he found no need to resort to violence to drive them out. In fact, Scripture quotes him as telling his followers that "this kind [of demons] can come forth by nothing, but by prayer and fasting" (Mark 9:29, RSV).

Are the insane likely to be possessed? Olga told the seminar that in some cases this *may* be true.

Q: Have you had any experience with insanity?
OW: Yes.
Q: Can you tell us something about that?
OW: In this particular case, the girl was possessed. Very often in cases of insanity there will be possession. A negative sensitive person can very easily be possessed by a person who once lived on earth, an earthbound entity who wants to continue earth experiences in a physical body. The earthbound spirit obtains possession of a person and controls the mind, then the unfortunate person is influenced to do things that the possessing entity wants done.

Then we have the other case of insanity which we call obsession, where the person becomes obsessed with an idea generated, apparently, by himself. The obsessed person is more difficult to heal than the person who is possessed. Possession is treated like a foreign element; the mind tends to reject it. Obsession is not treated like a foreign element, and the mind of itself makes no effort to reject it.

Olga is equally certain that there are beneficial agents who do not take over but who serve as helpers and guides from the other side:

The beneficial spirit does not possess a person but rather gives him ideas. The spirit would not take control. I speak of benevolent spirits— and doctors—from the other life. They would never possess the individual but would say, "We have been watching your progress and we find that if you will consider this suggested change you will do well— but you yourself must make the decision to alter your course." The beneficial spirits are the enlightened ones. It's the unenlightened ones who are the mischief-makers.

Much of the opposition among leaders of organized religions to psychic research grows out of the strong underlying fear of demon possession. Yet many younger leaders in the churches have come to the realization that whatever peril may be involved, it is even greater where we find ignorance, fear, unwillingness to face truth.

To the Worralls, the dangers lie not so much in the demonic as in the lack of widespread reliable information on the nature of psychic entities, and on their ability or inability to help or harm an individual.

A vivid picture of the Worralls' attitude toward this psychic reality, as they see and live it, is mirrored in the story of Doris:

Dr. Laidlaw: Have you seen human apparitions in the same spontaneous way, Ambrose?

AW: Yes, everything that we get is spontaneous. I have one case that I want to tell you about. This was the wife of one of our engineers. She was employed as a secretary. She became mentally confused and disturbed. Joe asked if I would consider seeing her. I was very busy at the time, and refused, because I know that mental cases are sometimes very long-range affairs; I told him to take her to a psychiatrist. This he did. In fact, they went for a year to a psychiatrist; he also took her to a minister and to a psychologist. None of them could find the real cause of her difficulty. She continued to experience periods of mental confusion. Joe came to me again and said, "Won't you see Doris just once?" I said, "Very well, I'll see her just once."

He brought her to our home the following evening. We sat in the living room and talked for an hour. Doris showed no sign whatever of mental aberration. I said, "I don't know what I'm supposed to do. I'm not a psychiatrist." Then I said, "Doris, come with me to the healing room." We went into the healing room where we sat in chairs facing each other. I said, "Just talk to me." She asked, "What shall I talk about?" I said, "It doesn't make any difference. Just talk to me."

She started to tell me about the office where she works and what went on there. I wasn't paying much attention to what she said. I was just sitting back waiting for an impression that would tell me what to do. Suddenly a mist passed over Doris and she disappeared completely from my sight. Sitting in the chair in place of Doris, I saw an elderly lady. Instantly I knew all that I needed to know to solve the problem. It just came to me in a flash.

I said, "Doris"—I still couldn't see Doris but I knew she was still in the chair—"I'm going to describe a lady to you and you can tell me who she is."

I described her and she said, "Oh, that's my grandmother."

I said, "Your grandmother raised you, didn't she."

She said, "Yes, my grandmother raised me. How did you know?"

"Don't worry about how I know," I told her, and continued. . . . "Your grandmother was a very good woman and always gave you good advice."

She said, "That's right, I never found any reason not to do as my grandmother said because she had good ideas and she never told me anything that wasn't right."

I said, "Your grandmother is dead, isn't she."

She said, "Yes, she died three years ago."

I said, "Do you know what your trouble is? Your grandmother is still telling you what to do. She is trying to help you. The other day when you were rearranging your furniture in the living room, and you wanted to put a chair in a certain place, something was saying, 'Don't put it there. Put it over in the other corner.' "

She said, "How did you know that? I didn't even tell my husband that, but this really happened."

I said, "That was your grandmother guiding you. She knew there was a draft in the corner where you wanted to put the chair and that anyone sitting there would have been sitting in a draft. She wanted you to put the chair in the other corner, where you finally placed it. Your grandmother is a wonderful woman; she means well but doesn't realize how she's confusing you. Now she understands what she's doing and she will leave you alone. You'll make some mistakes, but it's better for you to make some mistakes than to continue to be confused."

That girl has never had any trouble since. What I have been told by psychiatrists makes me think this kind of thing would be very difficult to discover because usually, I understand, psychiatrists are looking for some kind of traumatic experience or injury traced back to childhood. This was a well-meaning spirit, so closely attuned to this girl that, although she wasn't possessing her in the normal sense of possession, she was influencing her to do something opposite to what the girl had in mind, and although the ideas were good, the girl was getting confused. It is a very good illustration of what can happen to people. There was no evil intent, but the grandmother nevertheless caused trouble through her ignorance.

Doris' case reflects aspects of possession apart from the demonic. To those working with such situations, these facets are complex and require a special kind of diagnosis and intuitive knowledge.

How does one differentiate, for example, between real and false possession, the latter being possession by the individual's own ideas and confusions, mental and emotional?

Part of the answer, perhaps most of it, again has to be empirical. We are dealing in experience; the interpretation must be based on the validity of the one who reports that experience.

Some of the bewildering complexities involved are glimpsed in one brief extract of the dialogue following the Doris case:

Dr. Laidlaw: Ambrose, do you feel that cases of so-called multiple personality are cases of possession, such as *The Three Faces of Eve?*

AW: I've never read the book though I've heard much discussion about it, and I believe that people can take on different personalities. In fact I've seen it in people who are mediumistic, who take on any number of personalities, as many as forty in one case. It's not only that they claimed to be other personalities, they claimed to be actual beings. I knew one woman in England who, when possessed by a male spirit, would speak in a deep base voice.

OW: He took full control of her.

Dr. Laidlaw: It was temporary possession.

AW: That's right. Temporary possession. Arthur Ford goes into this type of possession when Fletcher controls him. Fletcher is a separate entity whom Arthur Ford knew when he was a child on earth.

Arthur Ford induces this type of control upon himself. When I asked him about it, he said, "I visualize Fletcher and I see him coming closer and closer to me until he becomes completely in control of me." He does it willingly. Eileen Garrett, I think . . . I've never seen her go into a trance . . . seems to be able to go into these trances at will.

Dr. Laidlaw: But there's a transition period of eight to ten minutes.

AW: Is it eight to ten minutes? Arthur Ford seems to take several minutes.

OW: There's only one entity . . .

AW: With him, yes, there is only one entity. Now Eileen, I think, had two, didn't she.

Dr. Laidlaw: She had four or five, but two, I think, were the main controls.

AW: I can see that where you have this harmonic condition an entity can take charge and . . .

Mr. Laurance: In regard to another entity taking over, we took video tape pictures in my home while this was occurring and we have the direct photographs on TV tape of the change in character of the person that was coming through, and it's extremely apparent that they take on completely the characteristics of the individual as a certain entity takes over. . . .

AW: There's another thing that I think electronics will show us some day—I refer to what is called etherealization. This is increasing the density of a spiritual body by some means to a point at which it can be photographed but can't be seen with the normal eye. However, a clairvoyant would see it.

The Worralls insist that often we open ourselves to entities by sheer carelessness in our thinking and acting. Our moral force is lowered, our own self-esteem, our esteem and love for others. What might be called the spiritual pores are opened to invasion just as the physical body is sometimes open to invading germs when the body is tired and in effect off guard.

A fragment of dialogue on demons:

Dr. Laidlaw: . . . in a sense they do, when you remember what we discussed in the case of a patient who was possessed. You can have a malevolent influence that can change personality.

OW: That's right, you can. Dr. Laidlaw is referring to the case of the deceased mother who continued to cause trouble after her death. I can sense either a possessive parent on earth or some other entity who has passed on to the other life but is still earthbound. These people, even though deprived of a physical body, are the ones who cause trouble.

Dr. Laidlaw: You'll be interested to know that it has been possible to block that entity off, thanks to you.

OW: I kept thinking about her, too. I visualized a wall of protection around your patient. . . . I had an experience just four years ago, a case of possession. A woman brought her son, about twenty years old, to the New Life Clinic. He kept saying, "Who am I?" When we invited the people to the altar rail for the laying-on-of-hands, the mother attempted to bring him forward to the rail but the boy wouldn't move out of the pew. After the church service the mother came to me and said, "I've come to get help for my boy, but he wouldn't go up to the rail." I looked at the boy and saw a possessing entity. I knew instantly that there was some shock when he was a youngster that allowed this possessing entity to take over.

Dr. Laidlaw: You saw it how, Olga?

OW: I saw the entity standing right behind the boy, blending into the boy's aura.

Dr. Laidlaw: You saw it in form?

OW: I saw the entity in form, an old man (an old man, I mustn't say that any more . . . when you get up into the sixties). He was probably in his fifties. [Laughter] I still think I'm about sixteen!

Dr. Laidlaw: It's all relative, Olga.

OW: I saw the spirit entity blending into the boy's aura, in complete control of the young man. There was conflict between the two of them. In an instant I knew that a shock had caused this entity to take possession. I didn't tell the mother that her son was possessed because I knew she wouldn't know how to accept this statement, and I'm sure the psychiatrist they were going to wouldn't appreciate such thinking. So, I said to her, "When your boy was about twelve or fourteen years old did he have anything happen to him that shocked him?" She said, "When my boy was fourteen years old he and his friends were fooling around with hypnosis. My boy was hypnotized and since then our son has not been himself." At the age of fourteen, this possessing entity took over . . .

Q: What happened to the boy?

OW: I mentally told the possessing entity to let the boy alone and go on his way. Then I mentally called on the experts in the spirit world that are working with me and asked them to take over. The young man and his mother did not return to the New Life Clinic so I don't know what happened to him.

In another case, a man and his wife came to the New Life Clinic. The man was an alcoholic. He said, "I don't want to drink, but something makes me drink." I tuned in and discovered a "drunk" in his aura. I told the man: "Why, you're just being a 'patsy' for this drunk." I described the situation to him and I said, "Every time you feel a compulsion to drink, you just tell that oaf to go elsewhere, that he's not going to use your body to get a good drunk on." He said, "Well, I'll be G . . . D . . . why, what do you know about that. . . ." and he went on in this fashion, indignant over the whole situation. . . .

Q: Did he know the person?

OW: No, before he was possessed he never drank intoxicating beverages. Then suddenly he developed a craving for drink and became an alcoholic. Three months later he came to church and said, "Mrs. Worrall, I haven't had a drink since I was here last. I've had the urgings but I've remembered what you told me. Boy, I got good and mad and I told that guy to go elsewhere."

Dr. Laidlaw: He did his own exorcising.

OW: He performed his own exorcism by becoming positive.

Q: Does this often happen with alcoholics?

OW: Yes, very often. They are possessed by earth-bound spirits who died when drunk and are still craving drink.

Among the techniques Olga and Ambrose use with invading entities are two approaches they consider important: help from non-malevolent spirits in the other world, and the "isolation" of possessing spirits:

OW: There are people in the other world who are experts in dealing with earth-bound spirits, and when we call on them they take over. Sometimes we can tell the earth-bound spirits that we are going to get help for them and that they no longer are to hover around the individual. That of course is when clairvoyance is very useful. . . .

There is so much to this that doesn't appear on the surface, those hidden factors that when understood can be very, very helpful in spiritual healing. When you get a patient and you suspect someone from the other life is exercising her possessive influence, just like that mother who was so possessive, you can isolate her with your thinking so that she can no longer touch the patient. . . . I like to "box such entities in," you know what I mean, mentally. If a woman comes to the New Life Clinic and says, "I'm having a terrible time with my sister," I will say, "Don't hate her. She doesn't understand. If she understood she wouldn't be doing these upsetting things to you. Just forgive her. Just rise above it."

Mentally I enclose the possessing entity in a force field, or whatever you want to call it, and at the same time I'm asking those on the other side to take over and to try to mentally impress that person to change her negative thinking, thus removing the desire to be destructive.

Voice: You put her in quarantine.

Psychic healers like the Worralls can serve as channels of help in cases of apparent possession, but results will depend on the cooperation of the individual and his desire to free himself. As with every other therapy, techniques of depossession are not always successful. Sometimes help comes too late, sometimes the possessing entities are too strongly entrenched, sometimes the will to be free of them is too weak.

Because of its potential threat to both mental and emotional stability, any person who feels that some kind of possessive force is involved in his own life or that of someone close to him should seek medical and psychiatric guidance. The answers to the nature and possible mechanisms of possession—and the extent of its role in the human personality—are still subjects of research. There is much that remains uncertain or unknown.

Regardless of individual cases, however, the field of possession, as unfolded at Wainwright House, presents a fertile field for collaboration between spiritual healing techniques and more orthodox psychoanalytic therapies, a collaboration that might enrich both fields and extend our knowledge of otherwise perplexing aspects of human behavior.

9
Shadows and Ghosts

There are witches still, we are told. There are hexers in Pennsylvania who for a dollar or two will put curses and spells on a client's enemies or business competitors. There is voodoo in New Orleans, Puerto Rico, and elsewhere. There are reportedly dolls for sale—and pins to stick through them—in sections of New York's East Harlem.

What is called "black magic" can best be described as the antithesis of so-called white magic. The latter deals in what is helpful to the community or the individual; it is a healing magic, in the metaphysical mind a balm in Gilead; it helps the sick to become whole, it lifts away the fear of evil.

Is evil an entity? Does it exist as actual, tangible, measurable reality? Can it bring harm to the physical body attacked by its force?

For centuries the polarization of white magic and black has been well known. It is shadows and sunlight, midnight and noon. On the one side is the good—helping, blessing, affirming this individual, this family, this home, this situation. Affirming God.

It may well be that such activities are foolish, meaningless, helpless, as some claim. But it is difficult to make a case that such affirmation does harm; on the contrary, even the most scientific minds are aware that affirmative thinking and believing in almost anything, including ritual, can affect affirmatively a problem situation.

On the opposite side of this metaphysical coin, black magic is considered as actually harmful in the negative force fields which it may set up in depressive thinking, feeling, believing, accepting.

Methods of so-called white magic often involve healing techniques, including the drawing upon the still little understood psychic healing forces. Whatever the technique, however, the force fields called upon are those of warmth, of love, of belief in life, in the essential meaning and dignity of creation.

AW: In Spain—I suppose I should say Old Spain—there were some people called the Salmadores and Ensalmadores and they were healers. They were credited with healing many kinds of diseases. One of the techniques they used was breathing on their patients. Some of these healers only touched their patients with fingertips.

Perhaps the most complicated circuitry is that brought about by multiple contacts between healer and patient. One example of this is taken from the Holy Bible. There we read that about the year 895 B.C. Elisha, when other methods failed to cure, lay upon the child and put his mouth upon the child's mouth, and his eyes upon the child's eyes, and his hands upon the child's hands, and stretched himself upon the the child, and the flesh of the child waxed warm. Here was complete coverage of the patient. I don't think you could recommend this in a public healing service, but here is an actual record of this being done and it was effective.

Now the question arises: Would this indicate that the healing power flow is in some way related to the sum of the areas of the points of contact, and that better results could be expected from laying-on-of-body, than in laying-on-of-hands, or the laying-on-of-feet? Science may answer this question some day. There are many other positions that could be assumed for contact between healer and patient. These are only limited by the imagination. Some could be beneficial and soothing, others could be irritating. All of this indicates a need for research to discover the proper methods.

The hex is part of the black side of the story—the spell that brings misfortune or disaster on someone else. In many Central American countries, in southern American cities, in the ghettos of New York and Los Angeles, black magic is a flourishing business.

Figurines with pins stuck through their plastic hearts are mumbled over in an effort to bring evil upon the intended victim of such action. Sometimes such efforts seem to result in doing injury. But more often than not, it is mere coincidence—or some actual physical harm done to the victim that is then pointed to as the work of the spell.

It appears true that psychic mechanisms exist and work in all orbits of psychic force, even those that are at opposite poles:

AW: We can see that science is gradually opening up areas which tie in with spiritual healing by showing the powers of reception and perhaps transmission capabilities of the human body, the human mind, or a combination of both, and that some day we'll understand the mechanisms and be able to set up the proper conditions and use them. . . .

I would like to leave the meeting open for discussion from the experts in all these different fields. . . .

Dr. Gardner: I think someone already asked this afternoon about the possibility of reverse action. . . . Do you believe in the possibility of black magic as the opposite of spiritual healing? Is it possible to knowingly injure someone with or without the person's knowledge?

AW: I think this is possible.

Dr. Gardner: Do you have any notion as to the mechanics of it?

AW: It would be easier without the person's knowledge in some cases, depending on the person. If a person had knowledge and understood how to combat it, he could set in motion the necessary force field to combat the destructive influence and it would then return to its sender—it would bounce back upon the sender. If a person is not aware of the mechanisms, he could be influenced quite possibly by this black magic without his knowledge because he wouldn't understand what was happening to him. In other words, if you understand the situation, you can combat it, but if you don't, there's no way to fight against it. It's like guerrillas in the dark of the night shooting at you. You don't know what you're fighting.

OW: We have never had any personal experience with the subject in question.

AW: We try to stay away from this type of thing because we don't want it to enter into our healing ministry, but I think there are plenty of records which show the evidence of destructive forces in operation.

Q: You think it's a real bit of deviltry then, actually?

AW: Yes, I think it's the use of destructive influences. For the people who believe in it, I think it is really destructive.

OW: We had friends visiting us, two Scottish women who had been governesses in India. They told us some of the extraordinary things they witnessed while living there. In one case, they were permitted to observe the practices of a medicine man, a witch doctor I imagine you'd call him. The witch doctor, for a certain price, would destroy the enemies of his patrons. The sheriff of that particular village told our friends, "We are utterly helpless against this witch doctor. He does things we can't combat. We just received word that a young man wants his enemy's hut burned and we're going to see what the witch doctor is going to do. Will you join us?" They observed the witch doctor as he set fire to sticks . . . and then using his magic powers he sent them on their journey through the air without any visible means of locomotion, in the direction of the poor victim's house. The lighted sticks arrived and set the hut on fire. This is the story, told by these two intelligent women who were respected for their maturity and keen ability to observe, and not given to superstition.

These women also told about a holy man who lived high in the mountains. While on government business, an English officer and his wife and daughter were stationed in this particular section. Shortly after their arrival, the daughter, about eight or nine years old, died. The child's body was being taken up the hillside for burial when one of the servants came running to the parents and said, "Sir, I know a holy man who could bring your daughter back to life." The officer said, "You bring him here." Almost within minutes, apparently by some psychic means of projection, the holy man appeared from high in the mountains. They said that he looked at the child and announced, "She will come back." He sat beside the child's body and began to chant, and the child stirred . . . she was alive.

Q: He was in his astral body?

forces can vary the weights of substances, and that the changes cannot be explained by gravitational forces. Significant differences in crystallization patterns after evaporation of liquid solutions have also been noted under different astronomical aspects of planets, and during eclipses. Could there be some correlation between planetary aspects and the incidence of success in spiritual healing?

The effects of magnetism on, and the passage of electric current through, living things have been observed to some extent, and results of these experiments could be helpful in studying the mechanics of spiritual healing. Electrostatic and magnetic force field intensities vary, and these changes could have a significant bearing on the success of spiritual healing therapy. Studies indicate a correlation between the intensity of the earth's magnetic field and psychical disturbances in some individuals. The World Meteorological Organization, a United Nations affiliate concerned with, among other things, the relationships between weather and human biology, observed that births, deaths, and accidents increase in rate of occurrence during high electrical activity in the atmosphere.

The following findings based on one million statistical facts may be of interest. During periods of high electrical atmospherics the number of deaths increased by 20 per cent; the number of births by 11 percent; the number of traffic accidents by 70 per cent; the number of work accidents by 20 per cent; and the number of mine accidents by 12 per cent over the rates on days of low atmospherics. Out of that same study came the following findings with respect to the sick. Brain patients showed a 30 per cent increase in complaints; amputation cases a 50 per cent increase, and chronic patients a 100 per cent rise in reports of pain.

Q: What kind of atmospherics?

AW: Electrical storms.

Q: Where was this study done?

AW: It was done at the World Meteorological Organization, a United Nations affiliate, and they wrote a paper and that's where I got these statistics. They may have much later findings now.

There are, Ambrose insists, destructive forces, but these in his opinion can work only when a person is susceptible to receiving them. As an illustration, he cited an instance that happened in Cleveland before he was married and in which he was involved.

He was living in a boarding house, and one night he attended a party of about forty people. A number of the guests were dancing:

AW: I took the job of playing the Victrola—you had to wind them in those days. Between changing the records, my attention centered on a lady sitting on the other side of the room. I saw a black cloud come through the wall and settle over her. She raised her hand to her forehead, and seemed to be in pain, and I thought, "I wonder what that cloud is." I left the Victrola and went around the dancers to her and said, "How do you feel?" She said, "I just got the most violent headache." The cloud was still around her, and looking into the cloud, I saw a woman's face.

I said to her, "Do you know a lady. . . ." and I described this woman to her. She said, "Oh yes, that's Mrs. So-and-So." I said, "Why would she be angry with you?" She said, "I didn't invite her to the party. We have too many people. I couldn't invite everybody. She heard about the party and was upset because she wasn't invited." I said, "Well, she is sending you the headache." She said, "She is?" And immediately the cloud disappeared and with it the headache. She had become positive and was no longer susceptible. But sitting there resting, idly watching the dancers, combined with the effect of the music, had brought her into a subjective condition just right for reception of the distressing thought projected by the disgruntled neighbor.

Dr. Laidlaw: This business of making an effigy and sticking pins in it can actually have an ill effect . . .

OW: Perhaps it can have an effect.

Voice: It's not the pins, it's the thought.

AW: They reinforce the thought by the physical action of driving the pins into the effigy.

OW: This indicates that an unsuspecting person can suddenly become ill and doctors would probably be unable to determine the cause. It is the psychic body that is being attacked, the results are reflected into the physical body.

Q: Is this necessarily a directed attack by someone or . . . ?

AW: Yes, directed attack.

OW: If you examine a patient and find absolutely nothing wrong, you can suspect that some thought is being projected at that person and the psyche is ill.

Q: Does the person sending this bad thought know that it is actually getting through?

OW: His whole objective is to get it through, sometimes he does not succeed.

AW: Usually when this is successful the sender has let the intended recipient know that he is the target for destruction by this method. The people that believe in this power are mentally conditioned to start receiving, especially if they believe in the power of the one who is operating against them.

Voice: Can hate do this?

OW: Hate can destroy.

These three words of Olga's are of deep significance. The psychic world around us, according to authorities like the Worralls, can involve forces that are either positive or negative. Much depends on our own emotional, mental, and volitional attitudes. Hate draws in the negative and destructive psychic force as love—compassion— draws the positive, the creative.

These too, the Worralls assert, are elements—functions—of cosmic law and order. Force fields of hate directed against another person or group can wreak great harm, they declare. Yet at the same time they point out that the characteristics of these fields, from a scientific point of view, have remained largely unexplored. Much of psychiatry, for example, concerns itself with the effect of hatred upon the hater. Too little time has been given to examination of just what can be the effects upon the object of such emotional force, especially when the target is unaware that he is, in effect, under enemy fire.

The Worralls themselves reported on one case which in its scope presented virtually the whole syndrome of challenge to the limited horizons of those scientists who find it easiest and safest to ignore or dismiss as unimportant any evidential experience regarding the paranormal.

In this experience of the Worralls, the issue is sharp and allows no room for equivocation. Either the Worralls fabricated the whole thing, deliberately distorted the facts, hallucinated it together—or it happened:

AW: A lady suffering from an incurable disease was brought to Wainwright House for treatment. The lady, accompanied by her husband, Dr. [O.J.] Bengtsson[2] and I went to an upper room and I treated the patient by placing my hands on her head. I sensed there was a restricted flow of blood to the left side of the brain. Dr. Bengtsson confirmed this, stating that a tumor in that location had been treated with X rays, which caused a reduction in blood supply.

During the treatment Olga entered the room, saying that she had been psychically impressed to leave the lecture being given by Eileen Garrett in the library and to join us in the upper room. I continued treating the patient as Olga took her seat. At this point Olga became clairvoyant. . . .

Why don't you tell it Olga, do you remember it?

OW: Yes, I do . . . I felt, through psychic means, that I was needed upstairs. I left the meeting and literally ran up the stairs. As I sat down to observe what Ambrose was doing, I became clairvoyant and saw standing next to the husband his deceased father. He looked like a duplicate of the czar of Russia.

I proceeded to give the husband a message, speaking in classical Russian, a language I had never heard spoken. The husband, amazed, said that his father had taught classical Russian in the University.

The man's father then said the wife was being hated by another woman—a distant relative by marriage—who wanted to destroy her, and who was cursing her.

2. Doctor of medicine; allergist in private practice in New York City.

Q: Was this distant relative dead or alive?

OW: She was alive.

Dr. Laidlaw: But the father gave you the message. The father was dead. When you spoke in classical Russian, did you echo what you heard him say or did he use your speech apparatus?

OW: No, each word that the father spoke to me I repeated as I heard it. In other words, as I was hearing him speak I was relaying one word at a time. It was the language the father always spoke at home because he wanted his children to speak, really, a forgotten language. The son understood and said, "That is my father." Even the enunciation of certain words . . . and as I heard them I tried to imitate them to the best of my ability, and it was the deceased father who said, "Your wife is being destroyed by hate."

AW: I want you to tell them about the watch and chain. This is a remarkable thing that came through.

OW: The father said, "You have my watch, but the chain that is on the watch does not belong to it. You sold the chain, and the chain that you now wear on my watch was given to you by one who loves you dearly, your mother-in-law." The man's father said, "If you will open up the back of the watch you will find an inscription with my name. It was given to me."

AW: The fellow took the watch out and upon opening it found the inscription in Greek.

Q: He had never known that before?

OW: He never bothered to open it up, and the chain that came with the watch was sold when they were fleeing. It was sold in Constantinople with other jewelry to obtain the money necessary to come to America. When he married, his mother-in-law presented him with a chain for that particular watch.

Q: Was there anything you could do in that case to help the woman?

OW: No, she died. Perhaps if he had been called in when the attack first took place, before the body was so badly destroyed, she could have been prevented from receiving the destructive thoughts.

AW: The father said that the relative was wishing that the wife would rot away.

Q: Now when a person is having such thoughts, are these just as effective if the person, who is having the thoughts, is dead and directing them to someone who is alive?

OW: I don't think that the person who is dead could have this effect. I've never experienced anyone from the spirit world cursing.

AW: But it is possible . . .

10
Search and Research

One achievement of the Wainwright seminars was to pinpoint the increasing need for modern scientific investigation of psychic phenomena, utilizing the latest instrumentation available. The advances of science itself have compelled many who toil in scientific and medical fields to seek answers to *things* that they know happen but for which scientific knowledge as yet has no answers in strictly materialistic terms.

Ambrose Worrall, in one of the papers he presented, pointed out the difficulty the scientist finds in bridging the dimensional gap between the study of the material and the nonmaterial:

> Science has gone far in its struggle to conquer the world of matter; has made some progress in its attempts to understand the laws of the mind; and is making an approach to the threshold of causation.
>
> From the viewpoint of science the study of the nonmaterial is extremely complicated. The problem of time and space in mental and spiritual processes has always been confusing. Where is the mind? Where is the spirit? And where is the soul? These are questions that the great thinkers have tried to answer.
>
> Democritus, as an example, believed that thought was located in the brain; anger in the heart; and desire in the liver. Plato was of the opinion that the mind was the active principle of the body and was responsible for controlling and working it. He did not understand how mind accomplished this function, but he divided mind into parts. The rational part he placed in the head; the finer impulses and emotions

in the heart; and the baser passions and appetites in the abdomen. Aristotle did not agree with Democritus and Plato, and declared that the mind was in the heart and not in the head.

Descartes pinpointed the location of the mind in the pineal gland. While we are still faced with confusing and contradictory views, one thing seems to be clear, and that is the improbability that mental states can ever be expressed in terms of matter. . . .

Is the nonmaterial merely a higher form of materiality—or are they two different things entirely? Can both be accepted without reservation as valid dimensions of the same divine creation?

Whatever similarities or dissimilarities are to be found in these dimensions, some efforts have been made and more are developing to test phenomena under laboratory and scientific conditions, the purpose being to seek to establish norms and variations from norms, factual and statistical data, psychic truth measured in the test tube as well as in the individual personal experience.

An example of this, involving Olga and Ambrose, is seen in an experiment conducted by Sister Justa Smith, biochemist of Rosary Hill College, Buffalo. Sister Justa's experiments, carefully controlled under laboratory conditions, were involved in measuring changes in enzymes in distilled water when there were magnetic fields involved and when there were no magnetic fields. In these tests, Ambrose held some of these specimens in his hands with results that Sister Justa considered of some importance:

AW: Sister Justa said she got something called a significant change when I treated enzymes by holding my hands in their vicinity. She said the change far exceeded any resulting from the effect of the physical magnetic field. . . . I found this very interesting. I've been trying for years to find some way of proving in a laboratory that the power that flows from a healer's hands can be measured. This seems to be one way of doing it.

Dr. Puharich: She has a beautiful experiment going. She's developed this over a period of three years where she has all the factors under control that measure the rate of hydrolysis of a synthetic substrate catalyzed by the enzyme trypsin; and it's a classic study. She's been studying the effect of electromagnetic fields in this system and has shown a statistically significant increase in the yield of this enzyme reaction, with a magnetic field as against a control with no magnetic field.

Having developed these control procedures, it was rather easy to apply it to a problem like this. She has also, as you know, been studying Estebany.[1] He first handles the bottled water, and she then puts the water into the reaction system. I really don't know what her latest results are.

AW: When she first mentioned the word enzymes . . .

Dr. Laidlaw: She's working with a qualitative measurement . . .

Dr. Puharich: I didn't know she had done anything with you, Ambrose. I knew she had worked with Estebany all summer, and if she has the results back now, I want to find out myself.

OW: Well, you see, when she asked me to hold this, I said, "This isn't the pure enzyme. There are two other things in with this." She said, "Oh no!" I said, "Well, there are three components: the enzyme and two others," and I don't know anything at all about chemistry. I've never studied chemistry. She said, "Why, Olga, that's right." She said there were two other components.

Dr. Puharich: Two other synthetics to stabilize the rate reaction.

Q: Doctor, what strength magnetic field is she using?

Dr. Puharich: I think about 10,000 gauss.

Q: And did she get an increase or decrease in the enzyme?

Dr. Puharich: An increase in yield of about twelve per cent.

AW: Yes, she said it had to be over ten per cent to be significant. Olga, you tell them what else happened . . . you only treated one specimen, didn't you? They took Olga off into another lab; I wasn't with her when Olga was doing this.

Dr. Puharich: Dr. Bernard Grad and I worked out the design of the experiment with her when I was up there a year ago in December.

OW: I'll tell you what happened. When we were sitting at the

1. Oskar Estebany. The Commission for the Study of Healing observed Mr. Estebany's healing gifts at Wainwright House in the summer of 1965. A report on these investigations is still to be published.

table talking prior to the experiment, I said to her, "But Sister Justa, you're going to work with blood also and you're going to make good discoveries with blood." And she said, "Why, Olga!" (She always says, "Why, Olga!") She said. "Sister So-and-So is just coming in this morning. She's going to work on the blood."

So then they left Ambrose behind and she and I went into a little room and she asked me to hold this after I told her about the two other things besides the enzyme—she asked me to hold another vial and she said, "Now this has . . . (and she told me . . . I don't know the chemical terms) and I want you to hold this." And I said, "No, I wouldn't hold this because you've already told me what was in it . . ." But I said, "I'll tell you what, why don't you try this with Ambrose?" I said, "I'm going to go out the back door so as not to come near Ambrose. I won't tell him anything . . ." So she took Ambrose into another room.

AW: Yes—Olga's right. She came and got me and took me to the other lab and we sat on opposite sides of the desk. She had a bottle, about three inches high and about an inch in diameter, containing something which looked like water to me. She put it in front of me. I said, "I won't touch it. I'll put my hands around it like I've treated other specimens. If I see anything, or hear anything, or feel anything, I'll tell you." I put my hands around it and I could feel the force field building up around the specimen and between my hands. As I looked down at the specimen, I saw a brown color like iodine stain. I said, "Has this bottle ever contained iodine?" She said, "Not to my knowledge." I said, "I see a color resembling brown iodine stain. I don't know what it means, but that is what I see." Then I saw a molecule (I never saw a molecule in my life, but what I saw I knew represented a molecule). It was transparent and dimensional, about two and one-half inches in diameter. It contained dark spots that made it look like the man in the moon. The display had two eyes, a nose, and a mouth, but the positions of the spots distorted the symmetry of the pattern. The bubble was also misshaped. I described what I saw. I said, "I don't know what it means, it's all out of shape, and I feel a little depressed with this substance." I don't remember more than the highlights of my clairvoyant impressions, but everything was taken down in writing. Sister Justa used an instrument with a probe which she placed between my hands. I believe she was checking the magnetic field.

Sister Justa left, and in a few minutes she came back with another bottle that looked exactly like the first one.

She said, "Let's try this one." I put my hands around it, and the first thing I saw resembled the surface of a pond and it was what I call electric blue in color. If you take a piece of friction tape in the dark and unroll it, you see light where the tape leaves the roll, that's the exact color of this pond. It was beautiful.

Next I saw a molecule. This time it was perfectly spherical in shape. It had a symmetrical dark interior pattern which I illustrated later in a sketch. I said, "I feel good with this." Again she wrote everything down. Sister Justa asked, "Would you like to know what was in those bottles?" and I said, "If you care to tell me." She said, "Well, that first bottle had damaged enzymes in it. The second bottle contained the pure native enzyme."

There are two ways to investigate the mind, Ambrose declares. One is by introspection, which is old, the other by experimentation, which is relatively new.

Ambrose and Olga believe that both methods must be used. They believe that the gifted seer can be of infinite value in this kind of research in understanding the force and uses of psychic energy. The spiritually gifted person can serve the scientific cause as a guide, as a teacher, as a direction finder of the spirit level or plane:

OW: We have thousands of letters from people whom we have not seen, but who have joined their prayers to ours at nine o'clock, telling us that wonderful things have happened during that quiet period—that a peace had come over them, that something happened to uplift the whole household. You can join us also.

Mr. Laurance: Each person has said almost the same thing here on the process of healing, that there are two basic parts: one is the generation of the energy forces, the healing forces, by one means or another (each one has a different technique for doing it), and the second part is the direction of the human energy to the individual who needs it, and Ambrose was just saying that you can use a computer to see that it is repeatedly directed as needed. But those are the two basic parts, and neither one of these requires the ability of the individual himself to be psychic and to see all these things.

AW: Sometimes you will feel the instant when this force flows to a patient. I get it many times when I am on the way to work in the morning. . . . I am open to influences in this never-never land that we're talking about, and often I will feel something going from me to a particular patient. The patient is suddenly impressed upon my consciousness and I feel something go from me, and in most cases at that particular time the patient is receptive and ready.

Mr. Laurance: Everyone involved can feel it.

AW: Yes, it can happen in prayer groups and all may feel this force.

Q: Ambrose, when you speak about physicians being trained for this—where would the training come from?

OW: It ought to come in medical school.

AW: I think we're a long way from that.

OW: I think that originally . . . who was the first doctor that started the practice of medicine? Who was the first engineer, where did he get his information from? He certainly didn't go to college. There had to be other sources of guidance, since there were no schools or colleges. Where did the first doctor learn how to use herbs and drugs for patients? He was receiving it inspirationally, he was receiving his guidance from the higher source that has all the answers. And being sensitive to that, he also used spiritual healing with his medicine. Do you see what I mean?

Dr. Laidlaw: The whole trouble is the faculties in the medical schools.

AW: They're brainwashed . . . that's the problem. But I think many who are psychiatrically oriented are dealing in this . . . dealing with things that you can't weigh on the scales. . . .

OW: How can a doctor become aware that there's much more? I thought that Dr. Arthur was really touching when she said, "Now, when I look at a patient across from me, I know that he is much more than just a body." After the first meeting, she said, "This has been extremely helpful to me and is going to help me understand many things that I couldn't account for with the training I had."

AW: We know about the electroencephalograph . . . that measures the nerve impulses from the brain. This is standard use. What I would like to see is two sets of this equipment set up at the same time on two different people, separated by a reasonable distance. Take readings, then bring the two people together in auric coupling range and see what effect it has on their responses.

Mr. Laurance: This has been done on twins. Mostly they respond the same.

Voice: I'm sure if you bring them physically in closer contact the fields intermingle.

AW: If you did that with a healer and the patient it might be particularly interesting to watch the patterns. . . .

Voice: I'm sure that when I'm near my wife I just reflect her patterns.

OW: I'm sure that's why you married her.

Dr. Laidlaw: The EEG doesn't give very fine distinctions, as a matter of fact. It shows a few waves of different characteristics.

Mr. Laurance: It's usually the quirks that show up.

Dr. Pahnke: What I was going to ask you is whether you have ever had your EEG measured while you were healing.

AW: No, I've never had it measured in any way, but . . .

Dr. Laidlaw: It would be a fascinating thing.

AW: It has possibilities.

Dr. Laidlaw: Eileen Garrett has had her EEG done in trance states, and hypnotic states, and normal states.

OW: Has it shown a change in each?

Dr. Laidlaw: To a minor degree. I haven't seen the records, but she spoke about it.

AW: I believe that we'll have to get a much more sensitive instrument than we presently have to give us what we want. If we can develop a more sensitive instrument for use in this coupling of people, it may bring out many important points.

The Wainwright dialogue disclosed that there are many experiments, either under way or projected, where the paths of science and the psychic world cross. These include the role of electricity and spiritual healing, heat therapy in cancer, electrical currents and healing, experiments with X-ray films and atomic patterns in healing.

The Worralls are not overserious about their gifts. They are spontaneous and fun-loving, and their experiments with force fields sometimes lead them into almost hilarious situations, as illustrated by the following incident:

AW: After some tests at Wainwright House to find out whether or not I was a dowser, Carlton Sherwood invited us up to his home. You know I'm an old skeptic ... but they said I was a dowser. Anyhow, Carlton said, "Let's go to a nearby farm and get a willow twig, and we'll do this in a real professional manner."

OW: Two engineers!

[*Laughter*]

AW: We went down to the farm and got this willow fork, then returned to Carlton's estate; I walked around holding the fork in the approved way and it moved up and down. I found I could trace what I believed to be underground streams by simply swinging the fork from side to side by twisting my body. I'd feel it dip down and then come back up again, and in this way I could find what appeared to be the center of the streams. I wasn't serious but was just making a big joke out of the whole thing. We were having fun.

After awhile Carlton called me over to a spot where there was a little square stone. He said, "Try it over here." So I put the fork over the stone and I said, "I feel nothing." Carlton laughed and said, "You're right over my artesian well. I've been getting water out of it for twenty-five years."

OW: Just then Ann comes out of the door and she says, "Carlton, we haven't any water!"

AW: And that well was dry!

Question: Did water ever come back into the well?

Carlton Sherwood: Yes, some did come into it (that's another story), but we decided to drill a new well and we weren't at all sure where it should be, so we decided to get in touch with Henry Gross.[2] Gross wrote back and said, "Just send me a rough map of the place." Later we sat down with him and went over the map, and he said, "This is a spot where three streams converge and, if you want it, there's at least sixty gallons a minute. If you do it right here, you'll get fifteen gallons a minute." So we did and we're getting twelve gallons a minute which is more than we need by far. This was all done without his coming to the place.

OW: He did it by psychometrizing the map.

Mr. Laurance: Map dowsing is becoming more prevalent than the regular dowsing. They use a map or drawing and go over it with a pendulum or rod. They have all kinds of techniques.

To paraphrase what Ambrose and Olga have been saying: There are force fields and laws that operate in the physical; there are force fields and laws that operate in the metaphysical. They work together, they interweave and intertwine; they work apart. But how and why and by what means are still to be fully understood:

AW: The word "forces" we have to take in a very broad concept. We don't want to get into the position of trying to argue the difference between energy and matter or the persistence of the elementary particles. That's on the frontiers of science, and we'll have to argue about that for many, many years. But I do believe that there are laws and conditions which have to be set up in order to have spiritual healing take effect. We read in the Bible that Jesus could do no great work there because of people's unbelief. It may have been just unbelief or it may have been something more than unbelief. It could have been a dynamic force of "You can't do it. I know you can't do it," which would set up a field in opposition to a spiritual healing force.

Dr. Miller: Ambrose and Olga were down at Atlanta a couple of weeks ago and I had an experiment in progress in which I was measuring the growth rate of a plant. My test plant had a growth rate of approximately 1 mil (1/1000 of an inch) per hour and was growing at a

2. Kenneth Roberts, *Henry Gross and His Divining Rod* (Garden City, N.Y.: Doubleday & Company, Inc., 1951).

constant rate. I showed Ambrose the plant and the recording apparatus. Later we went to another room where Ambrose sat at a desk and concentrated his thoughts on the plant. Within two hours, the growth rate increased to 6.1 mils per hour. The increased growth rate was 610 per cent of the original growth rate! The strange thing about it is that the acceleration was initiated, not when he concentrated, but when he walked into the room. The plant grew at the increased rate for about four days and then tapered off to its original rate.

As in many psychic-scientific dialogues, the final verdict is not conclusive; the results are not all in. They are indeed only beginning to come into focus. Perhaps the next great phase of psychic investigation will be in areas so far untouched. These may include areas today considered to be on the "way out" fringes:

Dr. Laidlaw: Before we go on, have the two of you felt that any of the cycles of the moon, for instance, have an influence on your work?

OW: I don't feel these influences, but I have observed with people who come to the New Life Clinic that those who are emotionally unstable, when the moon is full, experience nervous reactions, and that's when I get the telephone calls! They become either highstrung or very depressed, and we have one woman in particular who is perfectly fine until that moon starts to increase and then for those four or five days she really suffers. She cries, she feels depressed, and she says, "I don't know what to do; I have no reason for this, I have a wonderful family and yet this happens."

Dr. Laidlaw: What about your experience, Dr. Pierrakos?

Dr. Pierrakos: I just want to report on the work of Dr. Ravitz[3] and his studies in relation to the effects produced by cosmic forces on patients. These studies were conducted with special silver chloride electrodes developed by Burr and Northrop of Yale.[4] He observed that dur-

3. Dr. Leonard J. Ravitz, "Periodic Changes in Electromagnetic Fields," in *Annals of New York Academy of Sciences.* Vol. 98: 1144-1196, Oct. 30, 1962.

4. H.S. Burr and F.F.C. Northrop, "Evidence for the Existence of an Electrodynamic Field in Living Organisms," in *Proceedings of National Academy of Sciences.* U.S. 25:284-288, 1939.

ing the phases of the moon, especially the full moon, there were changes in the polarity as well as the quantitative aspect of the fields of the subjects relating to various emotional reactions. But I cannot give you specific information at this time.

The whole area of investigation of laws and force fields may hold more of the answers to the questions of psychic realities than any other avenue open to mankind and to the scientific community in particular. But for that community to play its role, it must, finally, learn to live with the charismatic individual, the psychic, the seer, and to work with the gifts or seeming gifts of such persons in evaluating exactly what is happening in these dramatic but still little-known areas.

11
Road Signs

The six seminar sessions were far more than merely pleasant get-togethers in a lovely home in Rye, New York. They were a quest for new highways of the mind and of the spirit, a search for directions into tomorrow.

Along the way, there were, indeed, eddies of thought, small excursions down sidestreets of ideas, possibilities, new explorations and developments. Some of them were sidetrips that proved to hold little promise. Other avenues could present real possibilities of breakthroughs.

Yet in these eddies and fragments of dialogue one glimpses also possible directions, road signs of the way to new understanding and to the elusive truth of these other planes, particularly in regard to energy and healing forces we do not yet understand, and in regard to the ways by which we may come better to understand these areas.

It is for us as individuals to recognize what seems to us valid and meaningful glimpses of truth—and to understand and use these gleanings affirmatively in our lives.

Fragments of talk that point a direction, a way, a mode of thinking, feeling, knowing.

One road sign in the possibilities of clairvoyance in a "healing" occurred between planes of reality. The healing here was directed to a family situation. A grandmother who had died appeared to Olga to plead for forgiveness from her granddaughter who was present. Olga served as a kind of intermediary in effecting this forgiveness in an emotion-filled experience.

This occurred when Ambrose was asked to lecture at a meeting of the Association for Research and Enlightenment, founded by Hugh Lynn Cayce, son of the mystic, Edgar Cayce, at Virginia Beach. During Olga's experience, Ambrose was with a group in another part of the building. Later that night when they retired to their quarters, Olga was simply too tired to tell him:

OW: . . . I said, "Darling, something happened that I can't talk about. I'll tell you in the morning." I lay in that bed and felt if I could only quiet down from the emotional . . . it is much harder than the physical experience. Then Ambrose called out, "Sweetheart, I see something. There's a woman standing by your bedside holding out a huge bouquet of white roses, saying in French, 'In gratitude.'" He described the grandmother . . . I said, "Oh sweetheart, I know what she means . . . I'll tell you in the morning."

Well, when we came downstairs in the morning, we met the granddaughter who was waiting for us, filled with joy and love for all. I said to the granddaughter, "My husband saw your grandmother standing by my bedside, presenting me with a beautiful bouquet of white roses and saying in French, 'In gratitude.'" The granddaughter exclaimed, "My God, grandmother's favorite flower—the white rose!"

"Dream Street" might be the name of another road the seminar participants glimpsed—the role of dreams as described in the curious poetry of Ambrose's psychic-scientific cosmos:

In studying psychic development the subject of dreams and their meanings often arise. Psychoanalysis has revealed that dreams are significant. They occur in the dream consciousness; this is a compartment of that mysterious house not made by hands, the abode of spiritual gifts. One characteristic of the dream consciousness is its ability to overcome obstacles which are unsurmountable in the waking consciousness. You can do all kinds of things when you dream which would be very difficult when you are awake. This is one of the characteristics of spiritual gifts. You know the answer almost before the question is asked. And how do you arrive at the answer? That is one of the mysteries which we might gain some knowledge of by studying dreams.

A little later in that fragment of dialogue Ambrose turned to the prophetic aspects of the avenue of the dream:

> . . . The dream-self has greater creative powers than the waking self, admitting, of course, that it is creating in a different environment. The conditions, environment, creatures, actions, results, created by the dreamer, are real to him, just as real as himself even though they can be proved to have a different time-space relationship to experiences of the waking state. Thus through a study of dreaming we may gain an understanding of the strange powers exhibited by those using spiritual gifts. I don't think this area has been explored in any great detail. I know they study dreams; I know they study spiritual gifts, but the tie-in between them I think could be explored much more.
>
> Prophetic dreams have been documented, and the events foretold have come to pass in exact detail many months later. This has also been accomplished by spiritual gifts outside of the dream state, so we can see the similarity of operation. It is possible to open the door to spiritual development by willing yourself to dream of a future event. If you are even partly successful in this it would be an indication of latent developable spiritual gifts. The only way to find out if this is the way for you is to work at it, keep records and develop your interpretation of personal dreams, for sometimes the future events are cunningly disguised by the dream consciousness.
>
> This is just a suggestion of how you might test yourself.

In a summary on his own ideas and road pointers regarding spiritual gifts, Ambrose stated:

> In the gift of clairvoyance we often are shown symbols which must be correctly interpreted to be of value. Practicing the interpretation of dream symbols will be helpful in the future when you develop clairvoyance. . . . The most successful method of developing gifts or talents is to practice entering into the silence, wherein one can be sure of developing his native ability upon a high spiritual level. . . .

One of the most important road signs, however, points not to individual power but rather to increasing awareness that all avenues of the spirit—unless deliberately misused—are channels to higher planes and to higher reality, ultimately leading to the power men call God.

Olga, in answering a question about healing, put this concept in her own often surprisingly simple expression:

Q: If you feel that you can't heal, what do you tell the patient?

OW: I don't tell the patient anything because I don't know whether I can or cannot.

Voice: I thought you said that sometimes you can't.

OW: Oh no, no, no! When a person comes to the clinic, we always say that *we* cannot heal anyone, it is God who does the healing; that all we can offer is our prayers and our love; that every service is an experiment and if they want to join in the experiment, wonderful; but that we cannot promise anything. It's all up to them. I would never tell a person I can't help him, but I would say, "I am not God. All I can do is pray for you."

But on the paths of reality, material or ethereal, there is also the question of time, what it is, how it fits into the mosaic of what we know and do not know. There are some who talk of "whole time" by which eternity becomes a tapestry in which past, present, and future are one, all of it there, to know and see if we will only understand.

Yet in truth man knows little of what he really means by time. Some hint, some glimpse of this, too, was seen at one seminar session in a scattering of road signs, some of which seemed to point to the East:

Mr. Louis Mobley:[1] . . . a newly discovered relationship between Buddhism and modern theology. I'm not a student of Zen, but I understand one element in Zen Buddhism is the idea of the ever-present

1. Staff associate in Public Affairs, Executive Development Department, IBM Corporation, Sands Point, N.Y.

Now, whereas traditional theology has been looked upon in terms of Hebrew revelation, namely, the sequential unfolding of events which has tended to mould our way of thinking of the real world. The new element is backing away from the idea of sequence and cause and effect in a sequential time sense. Rather than "a" causes "b" causes "c" *ad infinitum*—it is leaning toward the idea that a, b, and c are variables in the here and now, each of which is interacting on each of the others which, incidentally, John, is a pretty good description of systems analysis.

Mr. Laurance: Right.

Voice: It's interesting that Edgar Allen Poe expressed the same idea in the "Mystery of Marie Rogét" when he was commenting on God and he said, "With God all is now."

Mr. Mobley: I also heard a theologian say that Jesus literally meant it when he said that the Kingdom of God is at hand.

OW: Now. That is right. Not tomorrow.

Mr. Mobley: And not "out there." All of this kept coming to my mind as you talked about whole time.

AW: Yes, sequential time is a figment of the imagination, I suppose. But we would have difficulty in getting along without it.

Mr. Mobley: Cause and effect are very fundamental in traditional scientific thinking.

Cause and effect are sometimes seen in other perspectives, and the dimensions of space and time change when some infinitesimal speck of humanity, some animated fragment of divine spirit and divine gifts, reaches beyond physical cause to achieve spiritual triumph.

So we hear a beguiling fragment at Wainwright:

AW: Let me tell you another experience that I think would be very interesting. About three or four months ago Dr. F came over to our home. He took his bag back into our library and after awhile he said, "Come back to the library. I want you to do something." I went back there and he had the table covered with all kinds of bottles and samples. He said, "Each of these elements ties in to some star or some planet. I have figured out by the atomic numbers what I believe this ought to be. I would like you to hold each of these elements and tell me which planet or star these tie in to."

I know very little about astronomy; I know a little about astrology, which I studied at one time, so about all I know are some planet names. I picked up the nearest sample and said, "This is radioactive." Dr. F said, "Yes, it is, it is uranium." . . . You know, it was three days before I could get that tingling feeling out of my hands, even though he said it was very mild.

OW: You didn't tell me that!

AW: I didn't want to alarm you. I held each one of these bottles and samples and tied them in to a planet. There were some of them that Dr. F wasn't at all sure about but I tied them all in. In one case, I said, "This is tied in to a double star." He said, "Wait a minute, I'll read the names out to you and you tell me which one it is." He pulled a book of astronomy out of his bag and he read out all the names of the double stars. I said, "No, it isn't one of those." He said, "Well, that's all of them." I said, "I can't help it. There isn't one of those that ties in with what I feel." He said, "See if you can get something else." I sat back and waited . . . and then I said, "This is near the star Vega." He goes back through the book and he finds a double star which was not in the list of the double stars, and which was relatively close to this Vega. I told him, "That is the one." I was absolutely certain about it in my own mind, yet I have no idea how I could be certain at all.

Road signs pointing to areas we are only beginning to understand and explore, yet areas that have been known about and thought about since the beginning of time . . .

The kingdom of God that is within us all . . . And the kingdom that lies all around us in this magnificent universe . . .

Road markers to inner space—and outer space . . . Direction finders to the stars . . .

12
Meanings

What then are the meanings?

What final results or summations can be drawn from this discursive series of dialogues between physicians and the Worralls?

To this reporter one meaning can be summed up in the fact that new doors have been opened. There is a new understanding by doctors and by spiritual healers, a new interrelationship, perhaps even a new interdependence.

Even more importantly, many doors have been opened to a wide range of psychic areas to which the seminar road signs point. Communications have been shown to be possible between the disciplines and between individuals whose basic approaches are, or until now have been, in direct opposition.

It is truly a thousand doors, a thousand channels. It runs wide-ranging across and over psychic healing but through every phase and variety of paranormal phenomena. Even the doors to interpretation of terms have only recently been opened so that we can begin to agree on semantics.

A second important meaning is the new acceptance in serious, meaningful terms of the psychic role. This was clearly indicated throughout the sessions. No longer is there an "other side of the tracks" approach to psychic questions. No longer are the issues dismissed as carnival sideshows and petty fakeries. It is agreed that there are frauds here, as in every other part of life. But these serious students of the physical and metaphysical are concerned primarily with examining what is valid—scientifically as well as spiritually—what is the nature and essence of psychic phenomena and what they mean to us.

During the concluding discussion the group focused on the formation of an organization to explore these new channels and roads, the newly opened world beyond the newly opened doors. However, one of the essential purposes of this organization would be to research into what is called "life energies." This would be a probe in depth of the life forces, physical, spiritual, psychosomatic, and psychic, as well as the force fields created by varied patterns of life energies at work.

Such an organization would signal a wholly new development, apart from churches, universities, scientific societies, psychic societies—yet composed entirely of persons of professional standing willing to give of their time and energies, training and experience, in a cooperative endeavor to find glittering new answers to old dust-encrusted mysteries.

The answer to the meanings of these seminars is thus found to be meaning itself. It is a new day in which all of us can explore questions that have long held mankind captive in his chains of superstition, fear, scorn, and ignorance, questions that too often—because of these chains—we have been afraid to ask.

As a result of these dialogues, certain facts emerge sharply—and in turn raise other questions to be answered.

"It is a new day," Ambrose insists, "in which we are at last able to explore questions without having to face the mockery of science, the church's fear of demonic invasion, or the cynicism and skepticism of a public that has waited long for facts it could rely on.

"It is the harbinger of a new era in which the truth all of us carry within ourselves can be brought at last into the sunlight of outer day and the timeless yearnings of all of us for truth."

We do not know why some people are healed in spiritual healing and others are not. But there is no question that many are healed by spiritual therapies, in conjunction with medicine and after medicine gives up.

We do not know why some persons are gifted with seeming healing powers and others are not. We do not know precisely how these forces work—particularly at distances from the patient. But we have empirical evidence that there are such individuals and that the forces do in many instances appear to have successful results.

We do not know how the mechanism of prayer works. But we know that it too appears in many cases to be effective in healing.

We do not know why some persons are apparently gifted clairvoyantly and others are not. But it appears from the records of the seminar that there are these gifted individuals.

Also established was the fact that these postulates could be accepted in large measure as a valid basis for future exploration.

Further, the seminars established that medical authorities, psychiatrists, and psychologists could work together with clairvoyants and mystics and those with psychic charisma in probing beyond the the known physical and chemical realities. In healing most of all, where so much is known and so much remains unknown, these sessions established areas where answers may well be had in the near future, where even some of the most serious illnesses may be healed with new and deeper understanding.

It is a hope only, not yet a fact. But the avenues have been indicated, the road signs and pointers are there, the possibilities for breakthroughs in new dimensions are emerging.

The relationship of all of these forces to our daily lives, to our health and well-being, physically, emotionally, mentally, and spiritually, is of incalculable importance to our future as individuals.

For what answers we dare to search for—what horizons we dare to cross—will determine ultimately the destiny of humanity on this earth.